MW00647350

PAWS
ON MY PORCH

ISBN: 978-1-941213-73-5

Cover photos: ©Shutterstock

Printed in the USA

Published by:
TGS International
P.O. Box 355
Berlin, Ohio 44610 USA
Phone: 330-893-4828
Fax: 330-893-2305
www.tgsinternational.com

TGS001072

PAWS
ON MY PORCH

PRACTICAL POINTERS FROM

Drover, Moses, *and all the rest*

by Gary Miller

author of *Shaking Hands with Mr. Parkinson*

Table of contents

Foreword 7

DROVER AND MOSES 11

Title	*Scripture reading*	*Page number*
Desirous Drover	Psalm 107:1-16	13
Domineering Drover	Acts 9:10-31	14
Driven Drover	Revelation 4	16
Dancing Drover	2 Corinthians 4:6-18	18
Moses and Sam	2 Corinthians 11:16-33	20
Multitasking Moses	Psalm 63:1-6, Psalm 119:145-153	22
A Predictable Pair	Daniel 6:1-23	23
Defensive Drover	Joshua 22:10-34	24
Disgusting Drover	2 Peter 2	26
Merciless Moses	Matthew 18:21-35	28
Disciplined Drover	Romans 8:1-4	30
Dependable Drover	Ezekiel 33:1-20	32
Deaf Drover	1 Kings 13:7-25	34
Dumb Drover	Esther 6:1-13	35
Moses the Mouser	Revelation 12	36
Moses in Conflict	2 Kings 6:8-23	38
Distracted Drover	Luke 9:57-62	40
Disillusioned Drover	2 Samuel 12:1-14	42
Moses Makes Tracks	Hebrews 10:23-39	44
Scratching Fleas	Romans 7:14-8:6	45
Dentulous Drover	Galatians 5	46
Desperate Drover	Ecclesiastes 7	48

Title	Scripture reading	Page number
Moses Makes Do	1 Timothy 6	50
Moses and the Marauder	Genesis 3	52
Derelict Drover	Isaiah 62:1–12	54
Drover's Discomfort	Matthew 7:1–5	55
Drover's Dermis	2 Timothy 4	56
Undeserving Drover	Luke 17:1–19	57
Pets on the Porch	Psalm 90	58
Drover in Death	Ecclesiastes 3	59
OTHER CATS AND DOGS		**61**
The Blame Game	1 Corinthians 13:4–7	63
Stretching Sam	Psalm 42, Psalm 43	64
Driven to Trust	Psalm 37:1–20	66
Smokey	Numbers 22:1–22	68
Reactionary or Responsive	John 13:1–17	70
Cost-Benefit Ratio	Luke 6:20–38	71
Protecting the Innocent	Judges 13	72
Discerning the Danger	Proverbs 22	73
The Careless Are Crushed	Luke 16:19–31	74
Wooing the Wrathful	Romans 12	76
High Ground	Philippians 2:1–30	78
Middle Ground	Deuteronomy 30:10–20	79
Common Ground	Acts 17:16–31	80
In from the Cold	Mark 2:1–17	82
Pepper's Philosophy	Esther 3	84
Pepper's Dilemma	1 Samuel 17:2–31	86
The Profile of a Hypocrite	Romans 2:1–16	87
Remember to Look Up	Joshua 7	88
The Harshness of Love	Revelation 19:11–21	90
The Skill of Listening	Nehemiah 8	91
What Amiga Cannot See	Genesis 1	92
The Language of Barking	Acts 19:23–41	94
The Language of Sniffing	Acts 9	95
The Language of Growling	1 Samuel 20:24–34	96

Title	Scripture reading	Page number
The Language of Purring	2 Corinthians 1	98

OTHER ANIMALS, BIRDS, AND INSECTS **101**

Title	Scripture reading	Page number
Invaders	Acts 5:1–16	103
Food Chain	Luke 9:1–17	104
How to Take a Dust Bath	James 3:1–18	105
King Rooster	Proverbs 16:1–19	106
The Man and the Mosquito	Hebrews 9	108
Wee Winged Warriors	1 Samuel 25:2–25, 32–35	110
Takers and Givers	Matthew 10:1–16	111
The Bee	Genesis 45:1–15, 50:15–20	112
The Disciplinarian	Luke 9:51–56	114
Beautiful Boundaries	Proverbs 6:20–35	116
Prick Up Your Ears	Psalm 34	117
The Presumptuous Possum	1 Samuel 21	118
Blinders	Proverbs 5	120
Nest Building	Matthew 6:19–34	122
Who Owns the Barn?	Psalm 50	124
The Language of Crowing	1 Kings 20:1–21	125
The Language of Hens	Proverbs 15:1–15	126
The Language of Hooting	2 Kings 2:9–25	127
Dreading What's Ahead	Psalm 131	128

NATURE SETTINGS **131**

Title	Scripture reading	Page number
The Maple and the Vine	2 Corinthians 6:14–18	133
The Language of the Sunrise	Revelation 21	134
Save Our Planet	Hebrews 1	136
A Slimy Lesson	James 4:1–17	137
God of the Universe	Luke 8:22–39	138
The Leaning Pine	Matthew 25:31–46	140

Song Index 143
About the Author 145
Christian Aid Ministries 147
The Way to God and Peace 149

Foreword

Wise men and women are students of the world around them, taking note of things others ignore. King Solomon gleaned insight not only from the world-famous cedars of Lebanon, but also from "the hyssop that springeth out of the wall." Jesus drew startling truths from fishing nets, lumps of bread dough, and unwanted wedding invitations. Truly, wisdom cries in the street, and if we pay attention to the creation around us, spiritual revelations await us around every corner.

The simple lessons of creation carry remarkable sticking power. At daybreak one morning in my late teens, I climbed an old sugar maple at the edge of the marsh behind our house to pray and meditate. Dangling my legs from an overhanging limb, I watched a wood duck hen, nervous and alert, emerge from sheltering reeds into the open water below me. A dozen or more fuzzy ducklings trailed her in an untidy line. Before long, sensing my presence or some other threat, the hen gave a sharp, urgent call, and the family skittered for cover. But now the mother, though a better swimmer, brought up the rear, urging the stragglers onward and taking cover herself only after her last duckling reached safety. I'm a father of four now, and that little duck's example of sacrificial leadership still returns at odd times to encourage or rebuke me.

Collecting the nuggets of wisdom God sprinkles in our path requires habits of mindfulness that can be elusive in our noisy world. How often, busy and preoccupied with personal worries or grievances, do we miss opportunities to hear God's voice in creation, offering a solution to a nagging question, a healing perspective on a troubled relationship, or a warning against a subtle deception of the heart?

Clearly, God has enriched Gary Miller's life through his healthy habit of paying attention to little things, and the quirks of his pets will be familiar to anyone who has befriended a dog or cat. The bite-size devotionals take only a few minutes to read, yet each delivers a thoughtful observation on God or human nature that's worth pondering all day. Working with Gary on the editing process for this collection, I've been inspired by his delight in God's work and his avid pursuit of the Creator's wisdom in the world He has made—a reminder to keep my own eyes and heart wide open so that God's everyday object lessons can germinate and bear the fruit of righteousness in my life.

—Anthony Hertzler

All Things Bright and Beautiful

1. Each lit - tle flow'r that o - pens, Each lit - tle bird that sings
2. The pur - ple - head - ed moun - tain, The riv - er run - ning by,
3. The cold wind in the win - ter, The pleas - ant sum - mer sun,
4. The tall trees in the green - wood, The mead - ows where we play,
5. He gave us eyes to see them, And lips that we might tell
He made their glow - ing col - ors, He made their ti - ny wings.
The sun - set, and the morn - ing That bright - ens up the sky;
The ripe fruits in the gar - den, He made them ev - 'ry one.
The rush - es by the wa - ter We gath - er ev - 'ry day.
How great is God Al - might - y, Who has made all things well.
Chorus
All things bright and beau - ti - ful, All crea - tures great and small,
All things wise and won - der - ful, The Lord God made them all. A - men.

WORDS BY CECIL FRANCES ALEXANDER (1823-1895)
MUSIC BY WILLIAM H. MONK (1823-1896)

DROVER & MOSES

Desirous Drover

READ:
Psalm 107:1–16

My soul breaketh for the longing that it hath unto thy judgments at all times. —PSALM 119:20

Drover has learned some English. The highlight of each day is when the woman says, "Drover, are you ready for your treat?" He pricks his dog ears in immediate interest. The woman disappears into her house, and Drover listens intently. His body is rigid with anticipation. When he hears the rattle of the Purina Beggin' Strips bag, his front paws beat a rapid tattoo on the door step. His tail begins to wag furiously as saliva drips from his lolling tongue.

The psalmist of the Bible expressed his desire for God in vivid terms. Humans often experience their most intense longing for God only in the presence of suffering. Perhaps that is why a loving God permits His children to be afflicted and to grieve. He knows the trying circumstances of our lives can drive us to seek Him, to desire His Word, and to passionately crave its nourishment.

As the psalmist considered the plight of God's people—the wilderness, the wandering, the solitude, the hunger, the thirst, the fatigue—it dawned on him how this had all worked together for good. His heart burst forth with praise as he realized that this had all been part of God's leading His people in the right way. What soul-satisfying goodness from the hand of a loving God!

Drover snatches the strip from the woman's hand and moves off to a safe place where he will not be disturbed as he relishes his treat. His grasp of English does not include the ability to say, "Thank you."

Today we will relish God's Word, and God will be pleased as we think grateful thoughts and express them in prayer. Those around us will be encouraged when they hear us singing, and we will be doubly blessed.

As pants the hart for cooling streams
When heated in the chase,
So longs my soul, O God, for thee,
And thy refreshing grace.

—Tate and Brady

Domineering Drover

READ:
Acts 9:10–31

Look not every man on his own things, but every man also on the things of others. —PHILIPPIANS 2:4

Drover is not one of those dogs that roam the community. There is a powerful force that keeps him close to home. That force is his own selfishness. He lives in fear that his owner might pet the cat. If there is any head to be scratched or ears to be ruffled, Drover wants to be sure they belong to him. Sometimes when the man comes home from work, Drover rushes about madly, sending the cats scurrying for cover. Then he positions himself in the center of the walk, wagging all over, eagerly awaiting whatever attention his owner might bestow on him alone.

Of course, Drover is just a dog, so we excuse his self-centered ways. But how often do we humans act like Drover? In conversations with others, do we feel we can hardly wait until they finish so we can say our piece? Worse yet, do we interrupt? Perhaps we want to make sure we get the credit when we have done a fine job. We might volunteer for responsibilities that put us out front, but leave obscure and menial tasks for our brethren. Do we find it hard to compliment others, yet bask in praise that comes to us? Do we enjoy directing others but find it hard to submit to others' authority over us?

These domineering tendencies come from our fleshly nature. Let's leave these traits to Drover, while we Christians follow the example of Christ.

The path to fulfillment and happiness
Is to strive someone else's life to bless.

More Love to Thee

1. More love to Thee, O Christ, More love to Thee! Hear Thou the
2. Once earth - ly joy I craved, Sought peace and rest; Now Thee a -
3. Then shall my lat - est breath Whis - per Thy praise; This be the
prayer I make, On bend - ed knee; This is my ear - nest plea,
lone I seek, Give what is best; This all my prayer shall be,
part - ing cry My heart shall raise, This still its prayer shall be,
Chorus
More love, O Christ, to Thee, More love to Thee! More love to Thee.

Words by Elizabeth Prentiss
Music by W. H. Doane

Driven Drover

READ:
Revelation 4

Thou art worthy, O Lord, to receive glory and honour and power: for thou hast created all things, and for thy pleasure they are and were created. —REVELATION 4:11

Though Drover is just a dog, his life is nonetheless ordered by specific priorities. Chasing rabbits is high on his list of important things to do. While the man does his work in the field, Drover enthusiastically investigates nearby weed thickets and bramble patches. Panting happily, scrambling here and there, he probes and snuffles, following his keen nose ever closer to the hiding rabbit. He closes in, intoxicated by the hot scent of his quarry. When the rabbit finally explodes from concealment and sprints for safety, Drover rushes madly after it, yipping excitedly. Although he rarely catches his prey, he is never discouraged. He lives for the chase.

The man smiles reflectively. Wouldn't it be nice if his dog could apply that boundless energy to accomplish something worthwhile? But then he wonders what God thinks as He evaluates human lives. Maybe some of our priorities appear to God as Drover's priorities appear to the man. We have so many things that seem important to us. We rush here and there, filling our days with energetic enterprise. We tirelessly pursue our goals, intoxicated by the scent of success. Do we stop to evaluate the long-term value of all our urgent activity? Do our priorities help us fulfill the purposes of God?

When Drover chases rabbits, he is doing what God created him to do. God created us to bring glory, honor, and pleasure to Him. He is worthy! May we not disappoint Him.

Does the aim of our "game" seem odd to God?

I Have Decided to Follow Jesus

1. I have de - cid - ed to fol - low Je - sus, I have de -
2. The world be - hind me, the cross be - fore me; The world be -
3. Tho' none go with me I still will fol - low, Tho' none go
4. Will you de - cide now to fol - low Je - sus; Will you de -
cid - ed to fol - low Je - sus, I have de - cid - ed to fol - low
hind me, the cross be - fore me; The world be - hind me, the cross be -
with me I still will fol - low, Tho' none go with me I still will
cide now to fol - low Je - sus; Will you de - cide now to fol - low
Je - sus, No turn - ing back, no turn - ing back.
fore me; No turn - ing back, no turn - ing back.
fol - low, No turn - ing back, no turn - ing back.
Je - sus; No turn - ing back, no turn - ing back.

WORDS: VS. 1 AND 2 AS SUNG BY THE GARO CHRISTIANS, VS. 3 BY JOHN CLARK
MUSIC: FOLK SONG FROM INDIA / ARRANGEMENT BY WILLIAM J. REYNOLDS

Dancing Drover

READ:
2 Corinthians 4:6–18

Brethren, I count not myself to have apprehended: but this one thing I do, forgetting those things which are behind, and reaching forth unto those things which are before, I press toward the mark for the prize of the high calling of God in Christ Jesus. —PHILIPPIANS 3:13–14

Drover suffers many discomforts and indignities. Fleas nibble at his hide. Ticks burrow into his flesh. Mites pester his ears. Flies buzz around his head. Mats form in his fur. Sometimes when he sticks his smelly, panting muzzle into the man's face, begging for a bit of recognition, he is rebuffed for all his good intentions. However, none of these inconveniences dampen his enthusiasm for each new day or his exuberance for living. He refuses to hold a grudge. When the man walks to the barn, Drover is with him, dancing in ecstatic circles, panting excitedly, wagging his body from head to tail. He never seems downhearted or discouraged by the trials of living a dog's life.

Perhaps we pampered humans could learn something from Drover. How often do we become frustrated and upset when our day goes all backward and wrong? How grouchy do we grow when we don't feel well? How bitter are we when we suffer mistreatment or indignity? How discouraged do we get when we are misunderstood or falsely accused? How much do outward circumstances affect our Christian joy?

Drover will live his brief life and someday die like a dog. His understanding is limited, and his perspective is temporal. Our lives also may be brief, but our understanding is broad and our future is eternal. With the Lord as our strength, we can rise above life's setbacks and live our lives with godly joy.

Jesus, joy of living, Jesus, joy the best;
In our sorrows giving comfort, peace, and rest.

—Gotthold Schmid
(translated by John J. Overholt)

A Joyful Song

1. A joy - ful song of praise we sing, And thank - ful - ly we gath - er
2. From shades of night He calls the light, And from the sod the flow - er;
3. For noth - ing falls un - known to Him, Or care or joy or sor - row;
4. Then praise the Lord with one ac - cord, To His great name give glo - ry;
To bless the love of God a - bove, Our ev - er - last - ing Fa - ther.
From ev - 'ry cloud His bless - ings break In sun - shine or in show - er.
And He whose mer - cy ruled the past Will be our stay to - mor - row.
And of His nev - er chang - ing love Re - peat the won - drous sto - ry.
Chorus
In Him re - joice with heart and voice Whose glo - ry fad - eth nev - er,
Whose prov - i - dence is our de - fense, Who lives and loves for ev - er.

WORDS BY A. N. BLATCHFORD
MUSIC BY JOSEPH BARNBY

Moses and Sam

READ:
2 Corinthians 11:16–33

Let your conversation be without covetousness; and be content with such things as ye have: for he hath said, I will never leave thee, nor forsake thee. —HEBREWS 13:5

Moses was a yard cat. His was a life of freedom. He was free to prowl the premises hunting for frogs and mice. He was at liberty to tussle with his sibling or merely snooze on the sunny porch if he chose. All of the great, golden out-of-doors was his to enjoy.

Sam was a house cat. His was a life of luxury. He had every comfort a cat could want: soft, clean carpet underfoot, plenty of food in his dish, and a climate-controlled environment. The man's big, comfortable house was his to enjoy.

Moses and Sam sometimes sat at the same window, one on the outside looking in and the other on the inside looking out. The man could never be certain what was going on in the minds of his cats, but he thought he recognized a bit of envy reflected in those amber eyes.

Ah, contentment! How little it has to do with what we have or do not have. How much it involves an attitude of thankfulness and acceptance. The Apostle Paul testified, "I have learned, in whatsoever state I am, therewith to be content" (Philippians 4:11). He was content, though he had to flee for his life. He was content to suffer deprivation and imprisonment. He was content in spite of the infirmity of his flesh. He was content to endure hardness as a good soldier of Jesus Christ. Though his life appears far from ideal when measured against the modern "American dream," Paul had learned contentment.

It is not *where* we are but *what* we are that counts. Whether we are on the outside looking in, or on the inside looking out, let us be inspired to a life of thanksgiving and contentment.

Contentment is a choice we make, a way we live, a path we take.

It Is Well with My Soul

(faster)
1. When peace like a river attendeth my way, When sorrows like sea-billows roll;
2. My sin– Oh, the bliss of this glorious tho't– My sin, not in part but the whole,
3. And, Lord, haste the day when the faith shall be sight, The clouds be rolled back as a scroll,
What ever my lot, Thou hast taught me to say,
Is nailed to the cross and I bear it no more;
The trump shall re-sound and the Lord shall de-scend,
(cues: vs. 3 only)
"It is well, it is well with my soul."
Praise the Lord, praise the Lord, O my soul!
"Even so" it is well with my soul.
Chorus
It is well with my soul,
It is well with my soul,
It is well, it is well with my soul.

WORDS BY HORATIO G. SPAFFORD
MUSIC BY PHILIP P. BLISS

Multitasking Moses

READ: Psalm 63:1–6, Psalm 119:145–153

My soul shall be satisfied as with marrow and fatness; and my mouth shall praise thee with joyful lips: when I remember thee upon my bed, and meditate on thee in the night watches. —PSALM 63:5–6

Moses is gifted with the ability to do many things at once, even as he appears to be doing nothing at all. He lies quietly in the shade of a tree near the edge of the pond. A picture of relaxation, he may not move from the spot for an hour or more. Meanwhile, his human caregivers are hustling and bustling about, cleaning, mowing, trimming, picking up trash, and doing all the things humans do on a beautiful Saturday afternoon.

Moses understands that you can be still and still be productive. As he lies in the shade near the pond, he turns his head this way and that, his amber eyes missing nothing. He remembers his tasty meal of frog legs from last evening, and would be glad for more of the same for his next meal. He pricks his ears, analyzing every rustle, every ripple. Every once in a while he applies his rough tongue to the never-ending task of grooming himself. He has learned to relax and hunt and bathe, all at the same time.

Sometimes we humans rush around all day trying to get to the bottom of our to-do list. Finally we fall into bed, hoping for a good night's sleep, only to find that we are too tense to relax and slumber. Frustrated, we toss and turn. What a waste of time to lie for an hour or more, able neither to sleep nor to work.

The next time this happens, take a lesson from multitasking Moses. As you lie there, count your blessings, pray for everyone in your family, or frame in your mind the contents of a letter of encouragement you will write to a suffering friend or a newborn Christian. Like Moses, be still and still be productive.

To multitask, for wisdom ask.

A Predictable Pair

READ:
Daniel 6:1–23

And Jehoshaphat said, Is there not here a prophet of the LORD besides, that we might enquire of him? And the king of Israel said unto Jehoshaphat, There is yet one man, Micaiah the son of Imlah, by whom we may enquire of the LORD: but I hate him; for he doth not prophesy good concerning me, but evil. —1 KINGS 22:7–8

The man has been around dogs and cats most of his life. He knows Drover and Moses well enough to predict how each will act when he comes home from work. How surprised he would be if he came home one day and Moses came bounding out to meet him, dancing on his hind legs, jumping up and down, panting, and wagging his tail. And how strange it would seem if Drover merely fixed him with a frosty stare and then resumed licking his paw and rubbing his face. The man might even become alarmed, thinking his cat had lost its mind and his dog had fallen seriously ill.

Yes, pets are usually predictable, and it's good they are. Predictability can be a good trait in humans as well. The Old Testament describes Daniel as so predictable that his enemies were able to force him into a trap. They knew that if Daniel could be forced into a situation where he had to choose between his God and his life, God would come first. And Daniel did not disappoint them. He responded to their well-laid plans precisely as they thought he would.

Believers should be predictable when it comes to choices between right and wrong. We might be surprised how much worldly-minded people know about what Christians should and should not be doing. Do we surprise them by our rudeness, insensitivity, or coarse language? Do we startle them by our reactions to trying circumstances? May we never alarm anyone by seeming to have lost the mind of Christ and become spiritually ill.

Predictability:
When folks can know before the fact
Just how a Christian will react.

Defensive Drover

READ:
Joshua 22:10–34

If it be possible, as much as lieth in you, live peaceably with all men.
—ROMANS 12:18

"Bow, wow, wow!" challenged Drover furiously. What business did this strange white pickup have coming into his master's driveway? In truth, the arriving stranger had every right to be there, because Drover's master had asked him to come. But Drover didn't care what the facts were. He followed a simple policy: I will make lots of noise whenever I feel threatened.

In fairness to Drover, a dog really doesn't have the resources to investigate the intentions of visitors. But sometimes we humans start acting a little too much like Drover. We see a brother's action that looks suspicious, we feel threatened, and we start making lots of noise. We ignore the cardinal rule of communication: Seek first to understand, then to be understood. If we would only take a little time to listen, giving our brother the benefit of the doubt in the meantime, we often would learn that he meant no harm. The devil loves to create havoc in our churches by getting us to jump to conclusions about each other.

Today we read the account of a misunderstanding between Israel and the tribes on the other side of the river. Israel saw their brethren's actions as dangerous and threatening. As it turned out, everyone involved was concerned about following the truth. War was narrowly averted when all the facts came to light. Communication saved the day.

Defensive feelings can destroy communication and hinder mutual understanding. God has given us a level of ability, understanding, and accountability that Drover does not have. Let us use our God-given resources to maintain openness and understanding with one another.

Barking dogs make people run; empathy helps everyone.

Is Your Life a Channel of Blessing?

1. Is your life a chan-nel of bless-ing? Is the love of God flow-ing thro' you?
2. Is your life a chan-nel of bless-ing? Is it dai - ly tell-ing for Him?
3. We can-not be chan-nels of bless-ing If our lives are not free from all sin;
Are you tell-ing the lost of the Sav-ior? Are you read-y His ser-vice to do?
Have you spo-ken the word of sal-va-tion To those who are dy-ing in sin?
We will bar-ri-ers be and a hin-drance To those we are try-ing to win.
Chorus
Make me a chan-nel of bless-ing to-day, Make me a chan-nel of bless-ing, I pray;
Rit...
My life pos-sess-ing, My ser-vice bless-ing, Make me a chan-nel of bless-ing to-day.

WORDS AND MUSIC BY H. G. SMYTH

Disgusting Drover

READ:
2 Peter 2

For the time past of our life may suffice us to have wrought the will of the Gentiles, when we walked in lasciviousness, lusts, excess of wine, revellings, banquetings, and abominable idolatries. —1 PETER 4:3

Drover was clearly pleased with his prize. He stood over it, tongue lolling and tail wagging. The man looked on in disgust. He was not happy with what Drover had dragged into his yard. Drover's trophy was the foul-smelling, rotting carcass of some creature that had met its end several days before. Oblivious to the man's distaste, Drover rolled on the carcass, squirming this way and that, drooling at the rotten odor, and savoring the feel of the decomposed flesh against his fur. The man turned away. He would deal with the carrion later, or perhaps Drover would take his treasure away and bury it. But as he went about his work, he thought about what he had seen. He had heard that the worse something smells to a human, the better it smells to a dog.

Would it also be true, he wondered, to say that the better something smells to humanity, the worse it smells to God? He thought of what Jesus once told the Pharisees: "That which is highly esteemed among men is abomination in the sight of God" (Luke 16:15). Do we sometimes treasure the very things God detests? The man made a mental list of things men love: money, power, influence, prestige, recognition, pleasure, indulgence, and ease.

Oh, how sad it would be for God to turn away from us in disgust as we wallow deliciously in the rotting carcass of worldly pleasure.

"Father, help me love what you love and hate what you hate."

Adam's child by smut defiled, by sin enslaved, through Christ is saved.

Are You Washed in the Blood?

1. Have you been to Je - sus for the cleans - ing pow'r? Are you washed in the
2. Are you walk - ing dai - ly by the Sav - ior's side? Are you washed in the
3. When the Bride-groomcom - eth will your robes be white, pure and white in the
4. Lay a - side the gar - ments that are stained with sin, And be washed in the
blood of the Lamb? Are you ful - ly trust - ing in His grace this hour? Are you
blood of the Lamb? Do you rest each mo - ment in the Cru - ci - fied? Are you
blood of the Lamb? Will your soul be read - y for the man - sions bright, And be
blood of the Lamb; There's a foun - tain flow - ing for the soul un - clean, O be
Chorus
washed in the blood of the Lamb? Are you washed in the blood,
Are you washed in the blood,
In the soul-cleans-ing blood of the Lamb? Are your gar-ments spot-less?
of the Lamb?
Are they white as snow? Are you washed in the blood of the Lamb?

Words And Music by E. A. Hoffman

Merciless Moses

READ:
Matthew 18:21–35

For he shall have judgment without mercy, that hath shewed no mercy; and mercy rejoiceth against judgment. —JAMES 2:13

Moses didn't catch the finch to satisfy his hunger; he pounced on it because cats catch birds. And since he wasn't hungry, he didn't bother to kill his prey. Besides, to kill it would spoil his fun. He growled in anticipation; the finch struggled and cried piteously. Moses crushed a wing; then he let the bird flutter away, almost to safety but not quite. The bird shrieked again and again, desperate to escape. As its frantic efforts weakened, Moses demanded more action, tossing it into the air, extracting the utmost drama from the dying finch. What was idle play for the cat was a nightmarish death for the bird.

A few years earlier, when Moses was a kitten, he had nearly died an agonizing death himself. Trying to slip through a small hole in a wall, he had gotten stuck. No one knows how long he was there before the girl heard his weak cries and rescued him. Thinking of another baby rescued long ago, she called him Moses. But Moses didn't consider any of that now as he watched the dying finch with glinting eyes.

Jesus was instructing humans when He said, "Blessed are the merciful: for they shall obtain mercy" (Matthew 5:7). We have all experienced mercy—not only God's mercy, but the mercy of our fellow men. We wouldn't think of torturing a person or animal. But do we ever refuse to forgive? Do we give the "silent treatment" to someone who has hurt or angered us? Do we pass on unsavory information about others? Are we scornful and sarcastic? Do we belittle others? Do we mistreat those who are weaker than we? Do we feel someone's misfortune "serves him right"? If so, perhaps we are more like Moses than we think.

Divinely free His mercy flows, forgives my sins, allays my woes.

—Anne Steele, 1760

There's a Wideness in God's Mercy

1. There's a wide-ness in God's mer-cy, Like the wide-ness of the sea;
2. There is wel-come for the sin-ner, And more grac-es for the good;
3. If our love were but more sim-ple, We should take Him at His word;
There's a kind-ness in His jus-tice, Which is more than lib-er-ty.
There is mer-cy with the Sav-ior; There is heal-ing in His blood.
And our lives would be all sun-shine In the sweet-ness of our Lord.

WORDS BY FREDERICK W. FABER
MUSIC BY LIZZIE S. TOURJEE

Disciplined Drover

READ:
Romans 8:1–4

For whatsoever is born of God overcometh the world: and this is the victory that overcometh the world, even our faith. —1 JOHN 5:4

Drover approached his master with dread. His ears drooped and his tail sagged. His tongue darted worriedly about his chops, and his every aspect exuded guilt. The man needed to discipline Drover for his undisciplined behavior. Although Drover could not understand the scolding words, he felt the chastening tone of the man's voice. He had done wrong to carry the shoe off the back porch. Chewing the savory leather, saturated with the delightful odor of human feet, had seemed irresistible, but now he must reap the consequences.

The man's countenance softened as he observed the penitent dog. He knew what it was like to experience temptation. He understood many things about temptation that Drover did not. He knew that since the days of Adam and Eve, humans have experienced the classic pattern of enticement and failure: Look, lust, yield, and reap. He had also learned the formula for victorious Christian living: "Resist the devil, and he will flee from you. Draw nigh to God, and he will draw nigh to you" (James 4:7).

Drover's disobedience resulted in a tattered shoe and an irritated master, but when people disobey God, the consequences reach much further. Satan has declared war on God, and his objective is to snatch the souls of men and women from the hollow of God's hand. Temptation is the tool he uses to accomplish this goal.

God leaves the matter entirely up to us. He has given us the Bible, which shows us the path to victory. He offers His Holy Spirit to guide us. He willingly forgives when we repent of our sins. We need not live in defeat. We can be overcomers today.

**When sin appeals, in prayer one kneels and Christ's power feels.
With lust he deals; then Satan reels, takes to his heels.**

Yield Not to Temptation

1. Yield not to temp - ta - tion, For yield - ing is sin; Each vic - t'ry will help you Some oth - er to win; Fight man - ful - ly on - ward, Dark pas - sions sub - due, Look ev - er to Je - sus: He will car - ry you thru.
2. Shun e - vil com - pan - ions Bad lan - guage dis - dain; God's name hold in rev - 'rence Nor take it in vain; Be thought - ful and ear - nest, Kind heart - ed and true; Look ev - er to Je - sus: He will car - ry you thru.
3. To him that o'er - comm - eth God giv - eth a crown; Thru faith we shall con - quer, Tho' oft - en cast down; He, who is our Sav - ior, Our strength will re - new; Look ev - er to Je - sus: He will car - ry you thru.
Chorus
Ask the Sav - ior to help you, Com - fort, strength - en, and keep you;
He is wil - ling to aid you, He will car - ry you thru.

WORDS AND MUSIC BY HOTATIOR R. PALMER

Dependable Drover

READ:
Ezekiel 33:1–20

So thou, O son of man, I have set thee a watchman unto the house of Israel; therefore thou shalt hear the word at my mouth, and warn them from me. —EZEKIEL 33:7

Drover pays careful attention to his surroundings. His twitching nose constantly samples and evaluates odors wafted on the breeze from near and far. His keen ears detect the faintest noises. Even when he sleeps, a part of him remains ever vigilant.

He meticulously gathers information. When the man arrives home from work, Drover performs a careful inspection of the vehicle, circling and sniffing, analyzing the scent as only a dog can. At other times he patrols the man's property, snuffling here, poking there, investigating his path and marking his passage.

He is quick to challenge any sight, smell, or sound that seems foreign or unfamiliar. Woe to the marauding coon, the raiding fox, or the prowling bobcat who wanders into Drover's territory. Stealthy indeed must be the invader who would escape his notice. Though the scope of his surveillance is limited to his master's property, Drover takes his job as watchdog seriously.

God has called us to be watchmen. Our sphere of vigilance encompasses our personal lives, our families, our friends, and our church brotherhoods. The Apostle Peter says the enemy against whom we guard walks about "as a roaring lion . . . seeking whom he may devour" (1 Peter 5:8). But for all his ferocity, our enemy also stealthily presents himself as an angel of light (2 Corinthians 11:14).

Alone, we are not adequate to guard ourselves against the enemy of our souls. We are surrounded by threats. We need strength and wisdom from God. We need the insight and support of fellow believers. Be alert to the marauding individualist, the raiding false teacher, and the prowling gossiper. Be aware that these and other wrong influences often come to us in the form of something attractive and beneficial. We have a charge to keep; may we guard it well.

When dangers hide on every side, and faith is tried;
Watch far and wide, clear open-eyed; in Christ abide.

A Charge to Keep I Have

1. A charge to keep I have, A God to glo - ri - fy;
2. To serve the pre - sent age, My call - ing to ful - fill–
3. Help me to watch and pray, And on Thy - self re - ly,
A nev - er - dy - ing soul to save, And fit it for the sky.
O may it all my pow'rs en - gage To do my Mas - ter's will!
As - sured, if I my trust be - tray, I shall for ev - er die.

WORDS BY CHARLES WESLEY
MUSIC BY LOWELL MASON

Deaf Drover

READ:
1 Kings 13:7–25

For this people's heart is waxed gross, and their ears are dull of hearing, and their eyes they have closed; lest at any time they should see with their eyes, and hear with their ears, and should understand with their heart, and should be converted, and I should heal them.
—MATTHEW 13:15

Drover has a hearing disorder. It is a serious problem—too serious for even the finest veterinarian to cure. The man knows of no medicine that will correct his dog's condition. The problem is known as "selective hearing." Here are the symptoms Drover displays.

When Drover is asleep under the porch, the sound of a spoon scraping leftovers into his dish will bring him to his feet in an instant; yet he seems unable to hear the sound of the man's voice ordering him to cease his challenge to a stranger or break off his pursuit of a cat. Once the stranger has retreated or the cat has found refuge in a tree, Drover's hearing returns.

Selective hearing is a dysfunction that affects humans as well as dogs. This impairment does not originate within the ear but has its roots deep within the mind or will. It becomes most noticeable when the thing said runs counter to what I like to hear. This is bad enough if it results in tuning out the voices of my family or my church, but it becomes critically serious if I tune out the voice of God. We have this problem if we find ourselves swayed by the faintest suggestions of worldly influence, yet unable to heed the explicit directives of godly authority.

Someday we will be called before God's throne of judgment where we will be judged according to what God said, not by whatever He said that we personally deemed important. Although Drover will probably never find a cure for his disease, God is abundantly able to heal this problem in humans. He will effect the cure by touching the heart, not the ears.

The Spirit calls today;
Yield to His pow'r.
Oh, grieve Him not away;
'Tis mercy's hour.

—Samuel Frances Smith

Dumb Drover

READ:
Esther 6:1–13

For whosoever exalteth himself shall be abased; and he that humbleth himself shall be exalted. —LUKE 14:11

Drover wore a path all the way around Prince Rooster's pen—evidence of an ongoing test of wills between the two. Drover considered himself the second most important creature on the place. Only the man was more important than he. On the other hand, Prince Rooster recognized no one as his superior.

Dozens of times Drover raced around the pen, feinting, barking, and biting at the wire that separated him and Prince Rooster. If it weren't for the wire, he could make short work of his foe. From his elevated perch, Prince Rooster crowed defiantly at his antagonist. He probably wasn't even aware of the protection the wire afforded. Neither pet was interested in any agenda other than his own.

From the man's perspective, Drover looked dumb and Rooster looked ridiculous. Certainly neither of them appeared important. *What does God think when He watches humans like me striving for preeminence?* the man wondered. *Do we look as ridiculous as Drover and Rooster when we jockey for jurisdiction, strive for status, and posture for prominence? How often do we exult in our own excellence, unaware that only the thin wire of God's preservation stands between us and destruction?*

There is only one kind of striving that will benefit us beyond this life: "Strive to enter in at the strait gate" (Luke 13:24). All our energy and passion is required for this objective. Striving against one another in competition for some manmade standard of importance is both futile and absurd. God placed us here to help one another along our course to eternity, not to compete with one another. Let Drover pursue his foolish antics, while we focus on the things that are important from God's perspective.

So much strength is wasted competing for status;
None's left to resist when temptation comes at us.

Moses the Mouser

READ:
Revelation 12

Be sober, be vigilant; because your adversary the devil, as a roaring lion, walketh about, seeking whom he may devour. —1 PETER 5:8

Moses is perfectly equipped for mouse catching. He is much larger and more powerful than the mice he hunts. His lightning reflexes, sharp ears, piercing eyes, lethal claws, and slicing teeth all contribute to his success. But when Moses goes mouse hunting, he does not immediately need his claws and teeth. First he goes to an area where mice are likely to be. He crouches and waits, motionless except for an occasional twitch in the tip of his tail. After some time of stillness, his patience is rewarded by the rustle of an approaching creature. Every fiber of his body tenses for what will come next. In one swift pounce, he will pin the hapless mouse with his razor claws. Ahhh . . . then will be the time for the slicing teeth!

But the mouse, though he is small and weak, is not defenseless. In fact, his greatest strength lies in his smallness, for this enables him to escape into hideouts where Moses cannot follow. The mouse is vigilant and cautious. He is well aware that he is no match for his enemy in paw-to-paw combat. He must stay out of the cat's deadly reach.

Like the mouse, we are small and weak, and we face a powerful, lurking enemy who is perfectly equipped for people catching. He is experienced and patient. Just as Moses does not show his teeth at first, so Satan does not immediately reveal the purpose of his temptations. Only after a person is deeply ensnared does the bitterness of sin become apparent.

However, we are far from defenseless. Our strength is made perfect in weakness. Our smallness allows us to escape for refuge into the secret place of the Almighty. God's power will keep us from our enemy's deadly reach.

But thou, beloved Saviour, art all in all to me,
And weakness will be power if leaning hard on thee.

—Frances R. Havergal

Under His Wings

1. Un - der His wings I am safe - ly a - bid - ing; Tho' the night
2. Un - der His wings, what a ref - uge in sor - row! How the heart
3. Un - der His wings, O, what pre - cious en - joy - ment! There will I
deep - ens and tem - pests are wild, Still I can trust Him; I
yearn - ing - ly turns to His rest! Of - ten when earth has no
Hide till life's tri - als are o'er; Shel - tered, pro - tect - ed, no
know He will keep me; He has re - deemed me, and I am His child.
balm for my heal - ing, There I find com - fort, and there I am blest.
e - vil can harm me; Rest - ing in Je - sus I'm safe ev - er - more.
Chorus
Un - der His wings, un - der His wings, Who from His love can sev - er?
Un - der His wings my soul shall a - bide, Safe - ly a - bide for - ev - er.

Words by W. O. Cushing
Music by Ira D. Sankey

Moses in Conflict

READ:
2 Kings 6:8–23

But I say unto you, That ye resist not evil: but whosoever shall smite thee on thy right cheek, turn to him the other also. —MATTHEW 5:39

The man could not be sure how Moses got the gash in his head, but knowing cats as he did, he suspected that Moses had fought with another cat during the night. And being acquainted as he was with Moses, he could clearly picture the fight in his mind: Moses is patrolling the backyard when the big yellow tom emerges from the shadows. Tom fixes upon Moses an icy stare. Moses glares and arches his back. Tom hisses. Moses yowls. The two cats spend several minutes circling, posturing, and seeing which one can produce the most terrifying sounds. When Moses judges himself at an advantage, he lashes out with unsheathed claws and a vicious scream. Tom leaps to retaliate, and the two cats merge into a screeching, clawing, fur-flying fray.

In some ways, human nature is not so very much different from cat nature. Our troubles often begin when we claim a territory and begin patrolling it. Our territory could be our reputation, our image, our realm of influence, our finances, or our personal liberty. Confrontation happens when we feel someone is invading our territory. Conflict escalates when we quarrel, try to outdo one another, and strive for the advantage.

King Solomon observed that a soft answer turns away wrath. Jesus pronounced a blessing on peacemakers. Followers of Jesus love peace, and much trouble is averted by following the way of nonresistance. Moses and Tom must suffer the consequences of following the cat nature; but we know better, and we are blessed as we follow the Bible way.

When people, like cats, start to bite and to scratch,
Their conduct will never with the Bible way match.

How Sweet, How Heavenly

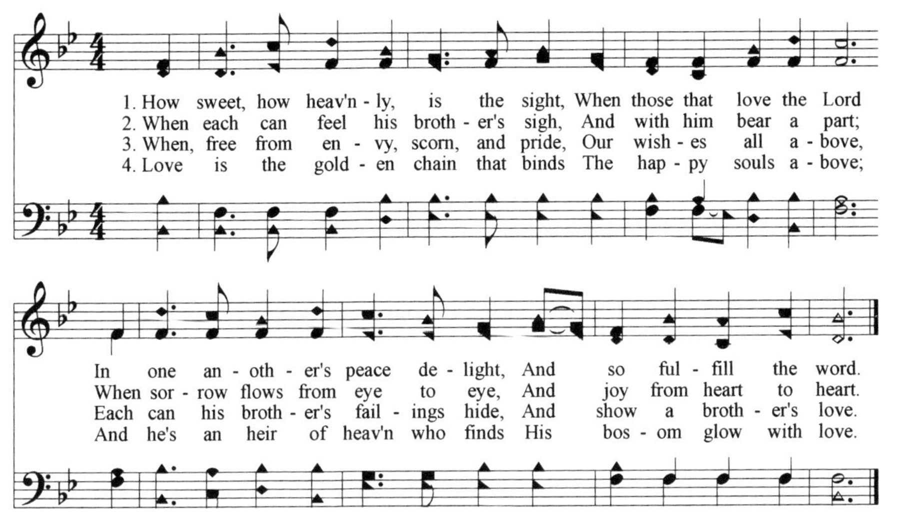

1. How sweet, how heav'n - ly, is the sight, When those that love the Lord
2. When each can feel his broth - er's sigh, And with him bear a part;
3. When, free from en - vy, scorn, and pride, Our wish - es all a - bove,
4. Love is the gold - en chain that binds The hap - py souls a - bove;
In one an - oth - er's peace de - light, And so ful - fill the word.
When sor - row flows from eye to eye, And joy from heart to heart.
Each can his broth - er's fail - ings hide, And show a broth - er's love.
And he's an heir of heav'n who finds His bos - om glow with love.

WORDS BY J. SWAIN
MUSIC BY WILLIAM B. BRADBURY

Distracted Drover

READ:
Luke 9:57–62

And Jesus said unto him, No man, having put his hand to the plough, and looking back, is fit for the kingdom of God. —LUKE 9:62

Drover pricked his ears. What was that sound? A raccoon? A bobcat? A thief? Or merely a stray puppy? With a bound he was off the porch. Striking his best watchdog pose, he prepared to roar his challenge. At that precise moment, a flea bit the skin at the base of his tail. Momentarily forgetting the threatening sound, forgetting that he was the watchdog, forgetting all but the stinging bite, he whirled to deal with the distraction.

We humans are often tempted with distractions that matter a great deal more than Drover's flea bite. Satan attempts to distract us from the straight and narrow way by lulling us with material comforts. He tries to sidetrack us by stirring up conflict in the church. Misunderstanding and suspicion are effective tools of distraction. We also tend to be distracted from eternal realities by the urgencies of daily life.

Many a wallet has been stolen by the thief who first distracted his victim. Satan has often stolen the advantage of Christians the same way. For example, some churches have sounded the alarm over the looming dangers posed by advancing technology, only to find that while they were busy keeping an eye on such obvious threats, subtle, divisive, worldly influences slipped in the back door. Was it all a clever distraction of the Evil One?

Drover does his best to run a one-dog security service, but he has no one to cover for him while he is being distracted. However, in a unified, spiritually minded brotherhood of believers, what one misses, another may see. This provides a tremendous benefit in our battle against evil. Above all, we need to keep our eyes on Jesus. May nothing distract us from our heavenly goal!

I'm pressing on the upward way; new heights I'm gaining every day.

—Johnson Oatman, Jr.

Higher Ground

1. I'm pressing on the upward way, New heights I'm gaining ev'ry day; Still praying as I'm onward bound, "Lord, plant my feet on higher ground."
2. My heart has no desire to stay Where doubts arise and fears dismay; Tho' some may dwell where these abound, My prayer, my aim is higher ground.
3. I want to live above the world, Tho' Satan's darts at me are hurled; For faith has caught the joyful sound, The song of saints on higher ground.
4. I want to scale the utmost height, And catch a gleam of glory bright; But still I'll pray till heav'n I've found, "Lord, lead me on to higher ground."
Chorus
Lord, lift me up and let me stand, By faith, on heaven's tableland,
A higher plane than I have found; Lord, plant my feet on higher ground.

WORDS BY JOHNSON OATMAN
MUSIC BY CHARLES H. GABRIEL

Disillusioned Drover

READ:
2 Samuel 12:1–14

This is my commandment, That ye love one another, as I have loved you. —JOHN 15:12

Drover can't figure it out. He goes out of his way to be winsome and charming. He greets the man by standing in the middle of his walkway. He dances on his hind legs. He wags his whole body. He pants as loudly as possible. He sloppily licks the man's hand at every opportunity, communicating his supreme devotion.

Meanwhile Moses, the worthless cat, sits to one side with frosty aloofness, making no effort to attract the man's attention. Yet the man scolds Drover while reaching down to pet the cat. To Drover, it doesn't seem fair.

Men and dogs don't think the same—or do they? The man pauses and studies his pets thoughtfully.

Men and dogs both have trouble seeing themselves as others see them. This opens up two areas of human responsibility. First, we need to be willing to receive admonition and correction from others. Such reproof can be hard to accept; we may feel picked on, or we may think ill of those who are trying to help us. However, to reject their input is to lose the benefit of their insight. Second, we need to kindly help those who need our direction. It takes humility, courage, and a caring heart to share a concern with a brother about a need in his personal life.

Clueless, Drover bumbles his way through life without the capacity to understand his own needs. We may not do much better without the input of fellow travelers on the road to eternity. Each of us is responsible to help others and to receive help.

Let us help while now we can,
Every burden to relieve;
As we bless our fellow man,
So a blessing we'll receive.

—Palmer Hartsough

While the Days Are Going By

1. There are lone - ly hearts to cher - ish, While the days are go - ing by;
There are wea - ry souls who per - ish, While the days are go - ing by;
2. All the lov - ing links that bind us, While the days are go - ing by;
One by one we leave be - hind us, While the days are go - ing by;
If a smile we can re - new, As our jour - ney we pur - sue,
But the seeds of good we sow, Both in shade and shine will grow,
Oh, the good we all may do, While the days are go - ing by.
And will keep our hearts a - glow, While the days are go - ing by.
Chorus
Go - ing by, go - ing by, Go - ing by, go - ing
Go - ing by, go - ing by, Go - ing by,
by; Oh, the good we all may do, While the days are go - ing by.
go - ing by;

WORDS BY GEORGE COOPER
MUSIC BY IRA D. SANKEY

Moses Makes Tracks

READ:
Hebrews 10:23–39

Of how much sorer punishment, suppose ye, shall he be thought worthy, who hath trodden under foot the Son of God . . . ? —HEBREWS 10:29

Moses stretched luxuriously on the smooth, warm hood of the man's pickup. Ahhh! This was perfect. From this vantage point, Moses had a commanding view of his surroundings. The sun warmed his body, and a light breeze ruffled his fur. He didn't notice that his paws had left dirty tracks and that his claws had scratched the paint. He didn't comprehend that the man had spent hard-earned money to buy this truck. As far as Moses was concerned, this was nothing more than a cat perch, which had appeared at this perfect place and time for his perfect enjoyment. What contentment! What tranquility!

A door slammed. The man's harsh voice grated on the peaceful scene. Moses jumped to his feet, alarmed. He couldn't understand the words, but he understood the meaning: it was time to leave—now! Moses scrambled for safety, leaving behind more scratches on the truck's paint.

The man looked from Moses to his truck and back to Moses. His irritation turned to thoughtfulness. He wondered how many times he had carelessly trodden underfoot something that someone else valued. Perhaps a few ill-chosen words had left dirty paw prints on someone's feelings. Perhaps a betrayed confidence had scratched a friend's emotions. These misdeeds could easily have happened through his neglect or carelessness, and he may have been unaware of the problems he'd left behind.

Worst of all would be to fall short of the grace of God and thus tread underfoot the Lord Jesus. Soberly, the man turned to go back to the house. As he went, he glanced again at Moses, who paused in his grooming just long enough to return his gaze knowingly.*

Who are you to judge your brother,
When you do the same thing he did to another?

—adapted from Romans 2:1

* This story is not an actual happening.

Scratching Fleas

READ:
Romans 7:14–8:6

But thanks be to God, which giveth us the victory through our Lord Jesus Christ. –1 CORINTHIANS 15:57

The flea made its way through the cat's fur, doing whatever fleas do, and causing Moses much itchiness. Moses applied the only remedy cats know—he sat down and scratched himself. The flea crouched low and hung on tightly as the cat pummeled his position with a rapidly scratching back foot. When the commotion ceased, the flea continued on his way, doing whatever fleas do. Moses is not able to reason his way to a more effective solution, so this flea-scratching routine happens again and again.

People are wise enough to know that if you want to avoid the itchiness of fleas, you have to do more than just scratch them. They understand that if you make the fleas go away, the itchiness will go away also. Yes, people are much smarter than cats—or are they?

"Tom" suffers much because of his hot temper. When he is provoked, he struggles mightily to suppress his angry reactions because he understands how foolish an angry man looks. "I guess my temper is my besetting sin," he says with a sigh after yet another failure.

Jesus said, "Come unto me, all ye that labour and are heavy laden, and I will give you rest" (Matthew 11:28). Tom can either continue scratching ineffectively at his anger symptoms, or he can turn to Christ and find rest in the real solution.

"Mary's" children often embarrass her by their undisciplined behavior. She scolds and pleads, but nothing seems to help. The Proverbs writer declared, "Correct thy son, and he shall give thee rest" (Proverbs 29:17). Mary can either continue to scratch ineffectively at the symptoms, or she can find rest by the use of loving, Biblical discipline.

God's Word provides solutions for people's problems. Without it, people are not much wiser than Moses the cat.

Hear the blessed Saviour calling the oppressed,
O ye heavy laden, come to me and rest.

—Charles P. Jones

Dentulous* Drover

READ:
Galatians 5

But if ye bite and devour one another, take heed that ye be not consumed one of another. —GALATIANS 5:15

Drover greeted Albert with open hostility. It was not important to Drover that Albert was the man's friend. Drover had his own rating system for evaluating the worthiness of his master's guests, and Albert had failed the test. Before the man or his friend could guess Drover's intention, Drover slipped up behind Albert and snapped at his leg, ripping his pant leg and grazing his skin.

The man was horrified by his dog's breach of etiquette and apologized profusely to his friend. But the nefarious deed had been done, and it could not be undone. Though Albert was gracious, the fact remained that his clothing was torn and his skin scratched. The man harshly scolded Drover, who retreated to a safe distance, keeping a wary, impenitent eye on his foe.

After Albert left, the man considered the lessons he might learn from the wayward dog. Dogs, he realized, are not the only creatures who employ arbitrary rating systems. Humans are perhaps even more guilty—hastily evaluating others, flunking them, writing them off, and not giving them a chance to prove their worth. While we would never destroy a pant leg, much less the skin beneath it, who of us has not been guilty of a sneaking attack from behind? This often takes the form of gossip or slander, an offense which Drover would never commit.

If we find that we have failed in these areas, let us humbly repent. Perhaps the one we have wronged will be gracious and forgiving. Let us make a practice of thinking kind, generous thoughts about everyone.

Let us do the kindly deed,
Let us speak the loving word;
They will spring like precious seed
In the garden of the Lord.

—Palmer Hartsough

Dentulous means "having or bearing teeth." *(Webster's New Universal Unabridged Dictionary)*

Let Him Have His Way with Thee

1. Would you live for Je - sus, and be al - ways pure and good? Would you walk with Him with- in the nar - row road? Would you have Him bear your bur-den, car - ry all your load?
2. Would you have Him make you free, and fol - low at His call? Would you know the peace that comes by giv - ing all? Would you have Him save you, so that you can nev - er fall?
3. Would you in His king-dom find a place of con-stant rest? Would you prove Him true each prov - i - den - tial test? Would you in His serv - ice la - bor al - ways at your best?
Chorus
Let Him have His way with thee. His pow'r can make you what you ought to be; His blood can cleanse your heart and make you free; His love can fill your soul, and you will see 'Twas best for Him to have His way with thee.

Words and Music by Cyrus S. Nusbaum

Desperate Drover

READ:
Ecclesiastes 7

Wherefore he saith, Awake thou that sleepest, and arise from the dead, and Christ shall give thee light. —EPHESIANS 5:14

The afternoon was warm. Drover dozed in the shade beneath the pickup truck. He heard the engine start. Something told him he should be moving, but he felt too deliciously drowsy to stir. Slowly, the pickup started backing up. Drover felt a crushing weight begin to press against his thigh. In an instant his drowsiness turned to desperation. He struggled. He rolled and flailed and raised a terrified cry. The driver heard and pulled forward, freeing Drover.

Although Drover did not suffer any permanent harm, he was thoroughly shaken. Tail and ears drooping, he walked slowly to his hideout under the porch. He needed time alone. He had lost all interest in chasing cats or barking at strangers. He seemed to understand he'd had a brush with death.

Sometimes we people get drowsy too. We sense danger and we know we should move, but we just don't want to bestir ourselves. When we become complacent, God has ways of getting our attention. Rudely awakened by a crushing circumstance, we desperately call on God.

Our response to God's deliverance should include a sober evaluation of our past deeds, our present involvements, and our future priorities. When God gets someone's attention, that person always experiences a change of interest. Former preoccupations no longer seem important as we realign our objectives to the standard of God's Word. We need time alone with God in prayer and meditation, and we need time to read the Bible in order to learn the mind of God.

Drover still sleeps under trucks on warm days, but now he is careful to move away in plenty of time. He has learned from his mistake. May we be as wise as he.

Awake to earth, asleep to God—how odd.
Awake to God, asleep to earth—new birth!

I Need Thee Every Hour

1. I need Thee ev - 'ry hour, Most gra - cious Lord;
2. I need Thee ev - 'ry hour, Stay Thou near - by;
3. I need Thee ev - 'ry hour, Most Ho - ly One;
No ten - der voice like Thine Can peace af - ford.
Temp - ta - tions lose their pow'r When Thou art nigh.
O make me Thine in - deed, Thou bless - ed Son!
Chorus
I need Thee, O I need Thee; Ev - 'ry hour I need Thee! O
bless me now, my Sav - ior; I come to Thee!

WORDS BY ANNIE S. HAWKS
MUSIC BY ROBERT LOWRY

Moses Makes Do

READ:
1 Timothy 6

And having food and raiment let us be therewith content.
—1 TIMOTHY 6:8

Moses lives a simple life. When hunger pangs stir within, he checks the cat dish on the back porch. If that is empty, he goes prowling for some hapless prey. When he is thirsty, he finds a puddle or a trickle to satisfy the demand. When he needs a bath, he diligently applies his built-in "washcloth." When he becomes sleepy, a rug or a cardboard box or most any nook will serve as his bed. Moses is content.

Moses does not worry about the future. He does not toss and turn in his sleep. He does not bite his nails, chew his lip, or develop shadows under red-rimmed eyes. Neither does Moses fret about the past. He does not cry over spilled milk, nor does he agonize over the mouse that got away. Moses is at peace.

Moses is genuine. He does not try to be something he is not. He does not try to be Drover. He does not try to be the man. He is content to be a cat, just as God made him to be. He does not gaze at his reflection in a puddle, wishing his eyes were blue. Moses is satisfied.

Moses is forgiving. He does not hold grudges. When Drover forces him to make an undignified escape up a tree, he waits patiently aloft until his antagonist loses interest. Before long, the two will be curled up side by side, sharing the rug for their afternoon nap. Moses is transparent.

Moses enjoys an uncomplicated existence. And though we cannot recommend a cat's life for humans, we might learn a lesson or two in forgiveness, contentment, trust, acceptance, and simplicity by observing his uncluttered daily agenda.

When the early morning breaking,
Slumber from my eyelids shaking,
Comes the blessed thought with waking,
I am in His keeping.

—Mrs. C. H. Morris

Be Not Dismayed Whate'er Betide

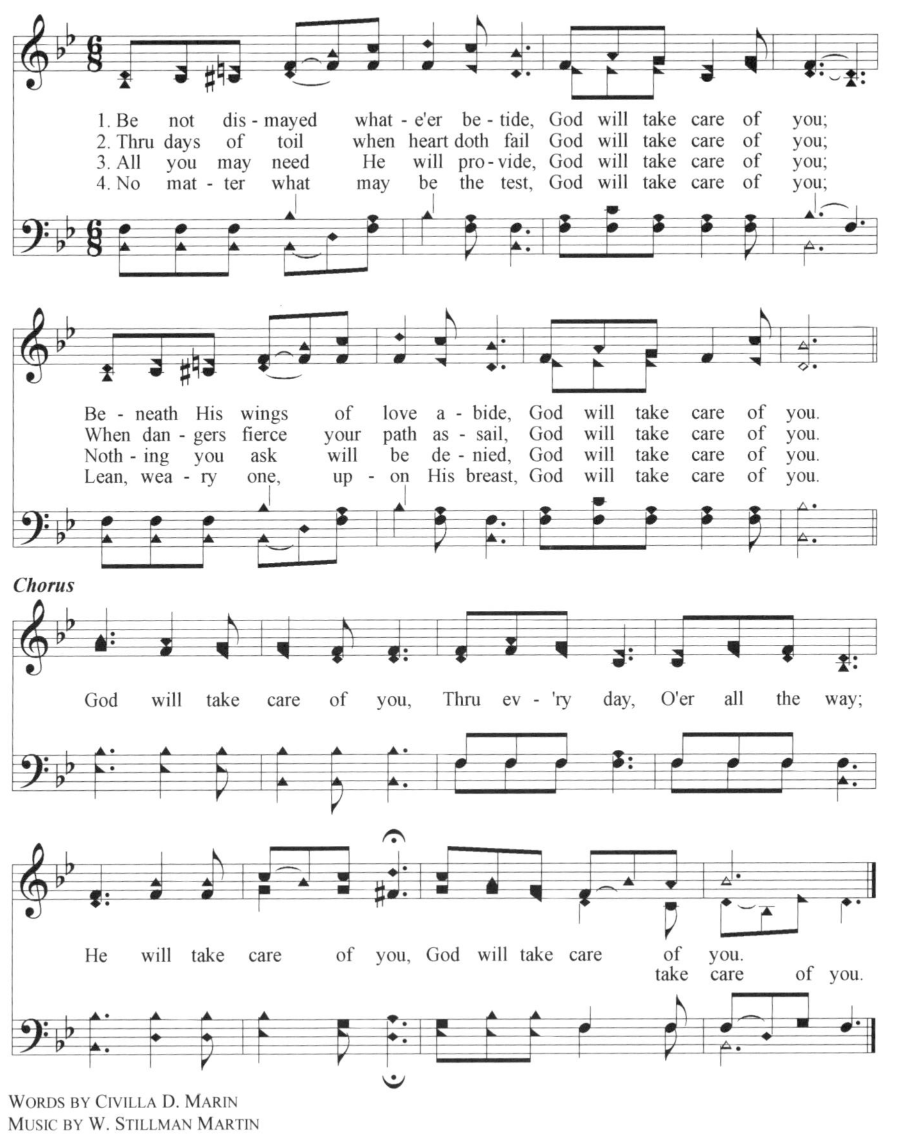

Chorus
1. Be not dis - mayed what - e'er be - tide, God will take care of you;
2. Thru days of toil when heart doth fail God will take care of you;
3. All you may need He will pro - vide, God will take care of you;
4. No mat - ter what may be the test, God will take care of you;
Be - neath His wings of love a - bide, God will take care of you.
When dan - gers fierce your path as - sail, God will take care of you.
Noth - ing you ask will be de - nied, God will take care of you.
Lean, wea - ry one, up - on His breast, God will take care of you.
God will take care of you, Thru ev - 'ry day, O'er all the way;
He will take care of you, God will take care of you.
take care of you.

WORDS BY CIVILLA D. MARIN
MUSIC BY W. STILLMAN MARTIN

Moses and the Marauder

READ: Genesis 3

Ye are of God, little children, and have overcome them: because greater is he that is in you, than he that is in the world. —1 JOHN 4:4

Moses the cat glanced fearfully over his shoulder. Life wasn't the same since the huge yellow tomcat had begun frequenting the neighborhood. He had ambushed Moses on a recent evening, and Moses had found that he was no match for the battle-scarred marauder. His screams of terror and yowls of pain brought the flashlight-wielding man from the house with hurried steps. As his rescuer neared, Moses was able to break free and run for safety. A moment later the traumatized cat found comfort in his box in the man's garage. As he listened to the man making loud, threatening people sounds, Moses instinctively knew that the man was his best hope for protection.

The man, however, felt more than a little frustrated. He wanted to protect his pets from this menace, but he didn't know when and where the marauder would strike next. In the following days, the big yellow tom would confirm the man's limitations, striking when least expected and outwitting the man at every turn.

We humans have an enemy who stalks us day and night, seeking whom he may devour. His ambushes are cunningly devised, and he strikes when least expected. We are no match for this powerful adversary, so we trust in our heavenly Father to keep us safe from his attacks. Unlike the man, our Defender is all-wise and all-knowing. He is well able to give us the power to overcome our enemy.

Today is a good time for us to commit ourselves once more into our Father's care, to request His presence throughout our day, and to renew our choice to live in obedience to His Word. Then we can face the day with confidence; there will be no need to look fearfully over our shoulders.

My faith looks up to thee, thou Lamb of Calvary.

—Ray Palmer

My Faith Looks Up to Thee

1. My faith looks up to Thee, Thou Lamb of Cal - va - ry,
2. May Thy rich grace im - part Strength to my faint - ing heart,
3. While life's dark maze I tread, And griefs a - round me spread,
Sav - ior di - vine; Now hear me while I pray; Take all my
My zeal in - spire; As Thou hast died for me, O may my
Be Thou my guide; Bid dark - ness turn to day, Wipe sor - row's
sins a - way; O let me from this day Be whol - ly Thine.
love to Thee, Pure warm, and change - less be, A liv - ing fire.
tears a - way, Nor let me ev - er stray From Thee a - side.

WORDS BY RAY PALMER
MUSIC BY LOWELL MASON

Derelict Drover

READ:
Isaiah 62:1–12

I have set watchmen upon thy walls, O Jerusalem, which shall never hold their peace day nor night: ye that make mention of the LORD, keep not silence. —ISAIAH 62:6

Pepper, an intelligent little Chihuahua with a shrill bark, recently came to live at Drover's house. Since Drover is getting older and isn't as sharp as he once was, he is learning to depend on his youthful assistant. Pepper quickly picks up on any sight, scent, or sound that is the slightest bit out of the ordinary. Pepper usually barks first; then Drover adds his deeper, more authoritative challenge when he becomes aware of the threat a moment later. This arrangement works out quite well, since it really doesn't matter who barks first, as long as every conceivable threat gets barked at.

However, sometimes Drover carries things a little too far. He has begun staying in his comfortable bed under the house, letting Pepper decide what needs to be barked at. This arrangement might seem to amplify the ferocity of his throaty challenge to his own ears, but to anyone listening from without, his barking sounds muffled and unconvincing. Besides, how can Drover know what he is challenging if he just barks because Pepper barked?

God calls us all to the sober responsibility of guarding against threats presented by the enemy of our souls. He expects us to be alert and to sound the warning to others. We must sit up and take notice when our leaders or fellow believers sound a warning. We must identify the threat and help pass the warning along. If we become too lazy to get up and examine our surroundings for ourselves, and we grow content to add our voices to the voices of others without knowing why, we fall short of being the perceptive, thinking Christians we ought to be. There is no shortcut for personal Bible study as a basis for making thoughtful applications to safeguard ourselves and those under our care from harm in the dangerous world in which we live.

Every watchman needs to know where is the danger, whence the foe.

Drover's Discomfort

READ:
Matthew 7:1–5

For the Son of man is not come to destroy men's lives, but to save them. —LUKE 9:56

The man listened, puzzled. Drover was barking. It was not his cat-in-the-tree bark; it was more like his stranger-in-the-driveway bark. But something was not right. Drover clearly understood his duty not only to make noise, but to stand rigid, head erect, ears pointed, and eyes alert, always facing the danger. But today Drover was not to be seen. He was under the man's house, barking. How could a watchdog do his duty from under the house?

The man called, and Drover appeared with his ears flattened and his head tilted. The man carefully examined him. As the man touched his ear, Drover winced. Ah, so here was the problem—ear mites. Drover understood that he was being attacked, but he did not understand from what direction. He knew his ears hurt, but he couldn't comprehend why. So he had retreated under the house to bark. The man took a medicine dropper and carefully put ear mite medicine in Drover's ear.

After Drover had gone his way, the man rubbed his chin thoughtfully. Do humans ever crawl under the house to bark? Perhaps they fall out of tune with God. They don't feel good. Their conscience troubles them because they are resisting the Holy Spirit. So they retreat under the house and bark.

They begin to find fault with others. They become critical, but their criticism is not constructive. Rather than addressing the concern directly, they talk to others who are neither part of the problem nor part of the solution. This is worse than barking from under the house, for it is not only ineffectual, but also destructive. When the disciples displayed such a spirit, Jesus rebuked them. He reminded them that He came to save, not to destroy.

Let us face danger out in the open, with eyes alert and conscience clear.

Have a critical bark? Come out from the dark!

Drover's Dermis

READ:
2 Timothy 4

For the time will come when they will not endure sound doctrine; but after their own lusts shall they heap to themselves teachers, having itching ears. —2 TIMOTHY 4:3

The man was concerned as he watched Drover's behavior. More and more, the dog sat scratching his flank with his back foot, or stood with his head twisted back, trying to bite at his itchy back. Patches of hair began to fall out where his claws and teeth had raked again and again. The skin was flaky and dry. When the man brushed Drover's fur, a back foot began its involuntary itching motion, thumping wildly, as if to assist the man in bringing this frantic irritation under control. One evening Drover just sat and howled his frustration. Something needed to be done, but what?

The man sympathized with Drover, having himself experienced the sensation of itchiness—the uneasy compulsion to rub, claw, scratch, and scrape to sooth a restless irritation of the skin. He understood that Drover's problem most likely lay in the dermis layer of skin beneath the surface. Scratching the outer layer, the epidermis, might provide temporary relief, but it was not likely to fix the problem.

As he considered the situation, the man realized that there is an itching problem more serious than Drover's. We humans sometimes have itching ears. Rather than hear the truth, we want to be told things that sound pleasant—things that temporarily relieve the symptoms of a deep heart ailment and make us feel good. Perhaps we even thump our feet or clap our hands in wild enthusiasm as our itch is scratched.

The problem becomes even more serious as we begin to reject messengers of truth and welcome teachers who bear the message of easy compromise. May the Lord continue to raise up church leaders who are not afraid to teach what we need to hear. Let us pay attention to those who are concerned about treating heart issues rather than mollifying surface irritations.

Those who itching ears do scratch
Will surely unsound doctrine hatch.

Undeserving Drover

READ:
Luke 17:1–19

So likewise ye, when ye shall have done all those things which are commanded you, say, We are unprofitable servants: we have done that which was our duty to do. —LUKE 17:10

Drover shivered. His allergy caused his skin to itch, and it had also caused him to lose much of his fur. He was sick and miserable.

Then there was Eliezer, the new kitten who didn't seem to realize that cats are supposed to fear dogs. He entertained himself with Drover's tail and even curled up on Drover's back at nap time. How can you chase a cat up a tree when he's sitting on your back? Drover's life had certainly taken a downward turn.

But now, as Drover huddled in the cold of night, he heard Eliezer's cheerful purring. The kitten bounded lightly onto Drover's back and curled up to spend the night with his big new friend. In spite of himself, Drover found Eliezer's warmth comforting.

It seems to me that cat-chasing Drover did not deserve to be comforted by a feline in his hour of need. But how much have I received that I did not deserve? I didn't earn the right to be born into a godly home. I didn't do anything to merit my parents' love and care. I am blessed with a good wife in spite of making some careless choices when I was young. Aside from the grace of God, I was helpless to receive forgiveness for my sins, yet Jesus shed His precious blood for me. It is beyond my understanding that I should be a fellow heir with Jesus, yet God has declared me His son by adoption. He has promised me a home in heaven if I am faithful.

My blessings are too numerous to list here, and I am not worthy of any of them. All things considered, I am more undeserving than my dog.

If you would find a humbling way
To face the dawn of each new day:
Just ponder how the Lord has blessed
In spite of our unworthiness.

Pets on the Porch

READ:
Psalm 90

So teach us to number our days, that we may apply our hearts unto wisdom. —PSALM 90:12

Eliezer is a young cat. He stretches his lithe body in a sunny spot on the back porch. He rolls over, purring contentedly, and splays his razor claws. Perhaps he is thinking of the hapless lizard he caught last night. What an entertaining time the little wretch gave him, until it was too tired and wounded to perform anymore. Life for Eliezer is an adventure.

Moses is a middle-aged cat. He sits at the edge of the porch and surveys his domain with cold eyes that miss nothing. Those eyes seem a bit disdainful as they rest for a moment on the young cat lying in the sun. Eliezer could benefit from some lessons on respect for one's elders. Moses rarely purrs or plays. Life for Moses is business.

Smokey is an old cat. He crouches near the cat dish, crunching a few morsels with his dull teeth. He looks fearfully at the world around him. He avoids Eliezer and Moses, sensing that they are aware of his weakness. Hunting did not go well last night. His stiff joints and dimmed eyes were no match for his darting prey. Smokey never purrs. Life for Smokey is survival.

The course of human experience flows from adventure to business to survival, much as a cat's life does. But God has provided for humans a pair of inner spiritual eyes that lift themselves in eager anticipation to their heavenly home, even as their physical bodies fail them. God has planned that the young respect and support the old, even as the old instruct and guide the young. These godly concepts are incomprehensible to the pets on the porch.

I'm but a stranger here . . . .
Earth's but a desert drear;
Heaven is my home.

—Thomas R Taylor

Drover in Death

READ:
Ecclesiastes 3

All flesh is not the same flesh: but there is one kind of flesh of men, another flesh of beasts, another of fishes, and another of birds.
—1 CORINTHIANS 15:39

The man stood watching Drover on the back porch as the dog vainly tried to soothe his diseased skin by licking the infected areas. He had long since scratched the fur away. The man had taken him to the vet, which was an ordeal for both man and beast. The vet had no certain answers about the skin problem, but he discovered that Drover also suffered from heartworms. To get rid of the heartworms would be expensive and risky, and would require many weeks of confinement for freedom-loving Drover. It just wasn't tenable. They'd tried bathing the dog and applying skin balms, but nothing seemed to soothe the irritated dermis for long.

Drover lay down and licked his skin until, exhausted, he laid his weary head on his paws. His breath came heavily. Then he began to squirm, and then he began licking again. He looked up, and his haunted brown eyes met the man's compassionate gaze. At that moment, the man reached the decision that he'd been dodging for weeks. If he loved this dog, he could not allow the suffering to continue. A tear slipped down his cheek, then another.

Drover was a loyal friend and a faithful watchdog; but finally, that is all he was, just a dog. He did not have a soul. In our society, dogs are taking the place of children in some homes. Couples are lavishing much of their affection and their wealth on their pets. This is not Scriptural, nor is it natural.

Drover never complained. He did the best he could with life as it came to him. Now his suffering has ended. His body lies in a small grave at one corner of the man's property, which he patrolled so vigilantly in life. It is a grave that will remain undisturbed on the resurrection morning.

A pet can teach us many things, its attributes inspire.
But like all life, an end time brings, and pets, too, must retire.

OTHER CATS & DOGS

The Blame Game

READ:
1 Corinthians 13:4–7

Finally, brethren, whatsoever things are true . . . honest . . . just . . . pure . . . lovely . . . of good report; if there be any virtue, and if there be any praise, think on these things. —PHILIPPIANS 4:8

It was beautiful and breezy the day King falsely accused me. When I opened the door and entered our shop, King was stretched out on the floor taking his nap. He blinked sleepily at me and saw that I was an acquaintance who had previously earned his permission to come and go at will.

Neither King nor I noticed the metal folding chair leaning against the wall near him. But when I entered the room, a gust of wind dislodged the chair and it teetered briefly before falling across King with a metallic clatter. Alarmed, King staggered to his feet and scrambled from beneath the chair, glaring at me over his shoulder and "woofing" as he retreated. To him, such an unprovoked attack was proof that I was no longer to be trusted.

I am not offended by King's false accusation, and I will do all I can to restore our friendship. I understand that King is just a dog, and it is gratifying to realize that humans with their superior intelligence would never jump to a false conclusion as King did—or would they?

Now that I think about it, I'm not sure our superior intelligence helps us much in this regard. The other day I saw two people whispering, and I was sure they were saying evil things about me. Also I left a message for the neighbor to call me, but he never did. Until I learned that he hadn't received my message, I was certain he was upset with me. I saw a man strutting down the street and thought, *There goes a very proud man.* Later I learned he walks that way because he lives with back pain.

How many beautiful days are spoiled by our ugly thoughts?

Jumping to conclusions keeps us slim;
We dance around a fact and grasp a whim.

Stretching Sam

READ:
Psalm 42, Psalm 43

O God, thou art my God; early will I seek thee: my soul thirsteth for thee, my flesh longeth for thee in a dry and thirsty land, where no water is. —PSALM 63:1

Sam, like most cats, has perfected the art of stretching. Waking from his nap, he uncurls himself, stands, and begins his stretch. He hunches his back, then drops his chest close to the ground, extending his front legs, splaying his toes, and protracting his claws. Next he pivots forward to stretch his back legs to their fullest extent, finishing with a flick of his tail and a toothy yawn. After such an elaborate stretch, Sam is limber and ready for action.

God created Sam with a supple body and lightning reflexes to catch darting mice or leaping frogs. Stretching is part of what it takes to keep his body in top condition. Of course, Sam does not understand any of that; he just stretches because it feels good to stretch.

We need to stretch too. Not a lazy, yawning stretch, but an earnest, heavenward stretch. We long to grow, but sometimes we do not put forth the effort to stretch and grasp all God has for us.

One way we can stretch is by personal Bible study. Skimming a page in a devotional booklet, then hurriedly reading a few verses, is not stretching. Take time to meditate, research word meanings, compare with other passages, and commune with God. Stretch toward God!

Charles Wesley expressed it well: “Father, I stretch my hands to thee, no other help I know.”

We must stretch because the Christian life requires our fullest effort. Poet Philip Doddridge penned these words: “Awake, my soul, stretch ev’ry nerve, / And press with vigor on; / A heav’nly race demands thy zeal, / And an immortal crown.” Let’s keep our souls limber by stretching every morning.

Draw thou my soul, O Christ, closer to thine;
Breathe into every wish thy will divine.

—Lucy Larcum

Awake, My Soul, Stretch Every Nerve

1. A - wake, my soul, stretch ev - 'ry nerve, And
2. A cloud of wit - ness - es a - round, Hold
3. 'Tis God's all - an - i - mat - ing voice That
4. Blest Sav - ior, in - tro - duced by Thee, Have
press with vig - or on; A heav'n - ly race de - mands thy zeal,
thee in full sur - vey: For - get the steps al - read - y trod,
calls thee from on high; 'Tis His own hand pres - ents the prize
I my race be - gun; And, crowned with vic - t'ry, at Thy feet
And an im - mor - tal crown, And an im - mor - tal crown.
And on - ward urge thy way, And on - ward urge thy way.
To thine as - pir - ing eye, To thine as - pir - ing eye.
I'll lay my hon - ors down, I'll lay my hon - ors down.

Words by Philip Doddridge (1755)
Music by George F. Handel (1728), Arr. by Lowell Mason (1821)

Driven to Trust

READ:
Psalm 37:1–20

Though he slay me, yet will I trust in him. —JOB 13:15

As the man worked in his field, his dog explored in the tall grass at the perimeter. Presently a rabbit sprinted out into the clearing, with the dog in pursuit. But the dog did not try to overtake the rabbit; he merely circled wide, heading his victim off and forcing the rabbit to run around the field in a wide circle. The man stood in the center, watching the drama unfold. The rabbit was slowing, tiring; the dog loped behind, prolonging and relishing the chase. Finally the exhausted and desperate creature realized that it had no other option. Contrary to the most basic instincts of the wild, it hopped to the man and slowed, allowing itself to be scooped up in the man's strong, tender hands.

The Old Testament book of 1 Samuel recounts a numerous instances of David fleeing from a deranged king who sought to kill him. Perhaps no other Bible character was pursued so relentlessly; and no other Bible writer has penned more eloquently his thoughts and aspirations of trust in God. When David was driven from society into the wilderness, he was also driven to trust God and to depend on Him for protection and direction.

Romans 8:28 assures us that all things work together for good to those who love God. *All things* includes both happy and sad circumstances, joy and sorrow, mountains and valleys, sunshine and shade. God sovereignly weaves these bright and dark strands together for our good and for His glory. One simple benefit of hard times—if we respond properly to them—is that they can drive us to trust God more fully.

Calmly commit your fate to the strong, tender hands of your loving heavenly Father.

When we're pursued by doubt and fear,
And all our options disappear,
We place our trust in His strong hand,
And know this for our good He planned.

I Am Trusting Thee, Lord Jesus

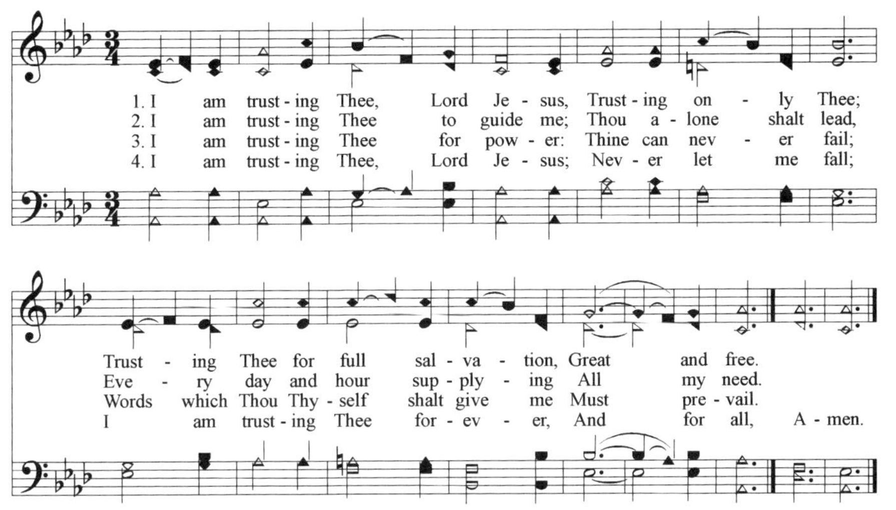
1. I am trust - ing Thee, Lord Je - sus, Trust - ing on - ly Thee;
2. I am trust - ing Thee to guide me; Thou a - lone shalt lead,
3. I am trust - ing Thee for pow - er: Thine can nev - er fail;
4. I am trust - ing Thee, Lord Je - sus; Nev - er let me fall;
Trust - ing Thee for full sal - va - tion, Great and free.
Eve - ry day and hour sup - ply - ing All my need.
Words which Thou Thy - self shalt give me Must pre - vail.
I am trust - ing Thee for - ev - er, And for all, A - men.

WORDS BY FRANCES R. HAVERGAL
MUSIC BY ETHELBERT W. BULLINGER

Smokey

READ:
Numbers 22:1–22

For the LORD God is a sun and shield: the LORD will give grace and glory: no good thing will he withhold from them that walk uprightly.
—PSALM 84:11

Smokey is getting old. His gray fur has lost its luster, and he carries himself stiffly. When it's cold, damp, and dark outside, he looks longingly at the warm glow of light surrounding the windows of the man's comfortable home. Sometimes the man or his wife will open the door a crack and let him slip inside to lie on the rug near the stove. How he enjoys soaking the warmth into his tired old bones. This is so much better than sleeping with the other cats in the garage.

But often the man refuses to open the door for Smokey. "You stay outside with Drover and Moses," he says firmly. This is hard for Smokey to accept. Even in the wind and cold rain, he stands outside rubbing his paws on the door and practicing his most pitiful meow. All the while, his fur is getting wetter and his bones are getting colder, but maybe, just maybe, the man will change his mind and let him in. Smokey could spare himself much misery if he would just accept the man's decision and go find a warm, dry bed in a corner of the garage.

How often do we, like Smokey, remain standing out in the rain and cold before the doors God has closed, pleading and hoping God will change His mind about something we want? How much more secure and comfortable we would be if we would cheerfully accept His will, knowing He would never withhold any blessing from us.

Prince of Peace, control my will;
Bid this struggling heart be still.

—Mary A. S. Barber

Prince of Peace! Control My Will

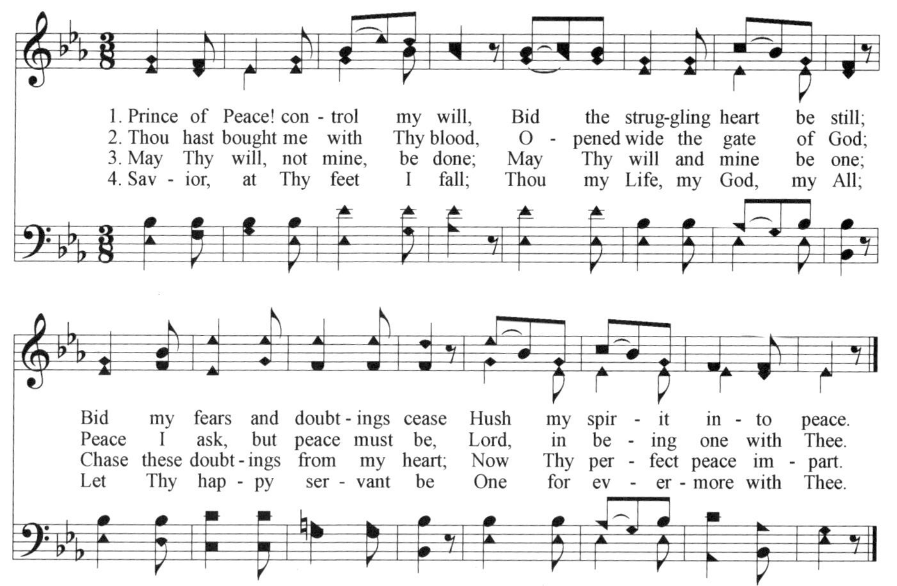
1. Prince of Peace! con - trol my will, Bid the strug-gling heart be still;
2. Thou hast bought me with Thy blood, O - pened wide the gate of God;
3. May Thy will, not mine, be done; May Thy will and mine be one;
4. Sav - ior, at Thy feet I fall; Thou my Life, my God, my All;
Bid my fears and doubt - ings cease Hush my spir - it in - to peace.
Peace I ask, but peace must be, Lord, in be - ing one with Thee.
Chase these doubt - ings from my heart; Now Thy per - fect peace im - part.
Let Thy hap - py ser - vant be One for ev - er - more with Thee.

WORDS BY MARY A. S. BARBER
MUSIC BY W. T. PORTER

Reactionary or Responsive

READ: John 13:1–17

If ye know these things, happy are ye if ye do them. —JOHN 13:17

A reactionary person acts within the context of whatever just happened—someone yells at me, so I scream back. The reaction is often far out of proportion to what the situation calls for. In contrast, a responsive person acts on the basis of broader principles. If I am responsive, and someone yells at me, I remember that a soft answer turns away wrath. Responsive people act thoughtfully.

Queen was a border collie who loved to please Jonathan, her master. "Go get the cow," Jonathan would command at chore time, and Queen would respond by darting away to the pasture. There she would sort out the cow from among the steers and gently bring her in.

One day Jonathan was gone and his wife needed to bring in the cow. "Go get the cow," she commanded repeatedly, but Queen refused to obey. Finally Jonathan's wife whacked the unresponsive dog with a stick. Queen took off for the pasture and soon returned with a wheezing cow. As soon as the cow entered the barn, Queen bolted for the pasture again and soon returned with all the steers at a dead run. Without stopping to catch a breath, she rushed back to the pasture and returned behind a herd of galloping horses.

Was Queen responding or reacting? Was she trying to make up for her failure to act or retaliating against her mistress for hitting her?

In today's Bible reading, reactionary Peter was like Queen, first refusing to comply and then trying to over-comply. Responsive Jesus calmly stayed on track with the original plan. We may be stressed, taxed, and tested today. Will we be reactionary or responsive?

Reactors go off at the circumstance trigger;
Responders are guided by precepts much bigger.

Cost-Benefit Ratio

READ:
Luke 6:20–38

Give, and it shall be given unto you; good measure, pressed down, and shaken together, and running over, shall men give into your bosom. For with the same measure that ye mete withal it shall be measured to you again. —LUKE 6:38

A cat caught a mouse. Not being especially hungry, she amused herself by tormenting the desperate little creature until it lay unconscious. Then the cat ate the mouse. This episode provided a few minutes of diversion and a midmorning snack for the cat, but it cost the mouse great suffering and the loss of the only life it had. By almost any standard, the cost-benefit ratio in the cat's act was far out of balance.

A criminal caught a victim and committed crimes against her, crimes that yielded him fleeting gratification but scarred the victim for life.

A teacher felt some small justification for replying to a student's question with sarcasm. She then proceeded to her next class and thought no more of the incident. But the student carried her hastily spoken words in a deeply wounded heart.

A young man captured the heart of a young lady. After a short time of dating, he found someone he liked better. He carelessly discarded the first relationship. What he considered harmless fun cost the girl a broken heart.

A mother took a job as a secretary even though her husband's income amply supported the family. She forfeited many hours of quality time she could have spent with her daughter. The girl passed from childhood through the teen years and on to womanhood without learning important principles a wise mother might have taught her.

When a cat exacts a disproportionate price from a mouse, she is merely doing what she is designed to do. But when a human makes choices with costs that outweigh the benefits, he is usually doing what God does not intend him to do. He who loves his neighbor as himself will see to it that others receive a fair benefit from their interactions with him.

Jesus showed the way to go; the best and highest ratio.

Protecting the Innocent

READ:
Judges 13

And Manoah said, Now let thy words come to pass. How shall we order the child, and how shall we do unto him? —JUDGES 13:12

The man and the woman acquired two beautiful kittens. These kittens came from a home where they had been loved, cuddled, and petted by cat-loving children. They were very tame and trusting, believing innocently that the whole big wonderful world had been created for their enjoyment. They never imagined for a moment any threat of danger.

As the kittens tumbled and scampered on the sunny back porch, the man stroked his chin and looked worried. How could he preserve their innocent trust, protect them, and at the same time integrate them with the realities of country life? Could they survive the learning curve that would introduce them to prowling neighborhood dogs and marauding tomcats?

Today, 370,000* beautiful, innocent, trusting babies will be born into our dangerous world. Some will be born to drug addicts, criminals, and murderers. Some will be born to agnostics, atheists, and Satan worshipers.

Some will be born to single parents in depressing poverty and squalor. Some will be born to parents who don't have time for them, don't want them, or even hate them.

But some fathers are pondering how they will protect and educate their vulnerable, innocent little ones while preparing them to live in a desperately wicked world. If you are a child or young person sitting with your family, listening to a godly father read these words, you are among the most blessed children on the face of the earth.

To protect a kitten is a good thing; to protect a child is infinitely more important. So fathers and mothers, ponder on, for eternity will bear testimony to your success or failure.

Train up a child in the way he should go,
That the way of God's kingdom he might know.

—adapted from Proverbs 22:6

*Current Census Bureau

Discerning the Danger

READ:
Proverbs 22

For when they shall say, Peace and safety; then sudden destruction cometh upon them. —1 THESSALONIANS 5:3

The man and the woman considered what to name their two new kittens, but considering the shortness of the little creatures' life expectancy, they decided to postpone the naming. It was the kittens' utter lack of fear that so endangered their lives; they had no qualms about automobiles, and they did not comprehend the dangers of crawling into the undercarriage of any vehicle.

Of course the man and the woman took every precaution they could think of to protect the kittens from their own lack of discernment, yet they knew that unless the kittens learned a proper respect for cars, they would not survive long in an environment where cars come and go.

Our communities have people of all ages, from infants to the elderly. The gray-haired men don't know everything, but the longer one lives, the more one knows—if he keeps his eyes and ears open. Youth know a lot too, but unlike the aged, a youth's conclusions have not yet been tested by time. Sometimes an older person sees a young person engaged in an activity that the older one knows from firsthand experience will cause heartache and perhaps even spiritual death.

In a world where adventure beckons and Satan lurks, we take every precaution we can think of to protect our youth. Yet we understand that unless our youth embrace God's truth, grow in wisdom, and develop their own discernment, they will not survive long in an environment where temptations come and go.

How do you teach a kitten about cars? How do you fortify your son or daughter to stand in the hour of temptation? Both questions are difficult, but Psalm 119:11 has the answer for the question that really matters. "Thy word have I hid in mine heart, that I might not sin against thee."

"There's danger ahead!" the watchman said,
And those with no dread are long since dead.

The Careless Are Crushed

READ: Luke 16:19–31

And whosoever shall fall on this stone shall be broken: but on whomsoever it shall fall, it will grind him to powder. —MATTHEW 21:44

The man was greeted by only one kitten when he stepped out on the back porch. *Where's the gray kitten?* he wondered. Later that morning he found its lifeless form lying crushed in the driveway.

The story was easy to piece together. Visitors had been there the evening before. The gray kitten must have crawled up onto the chassis of their vehicle. After a pleasant evening, the visitors had bidden the man and his wife farewell and had driven away. They never knew when a small gray kitten leaped lightly from the chassis and was crushed by the tires.

The man looked at the lifeless form and wished he could have done more to instruct the kitten of driveway dangers.

We want to teach our children about God and shelter them from the dangers of this world as much as we can. We want to tell them as much as is appropriate for their ages about avoiding the snares of temptations. Our goal is that each child learns to think for himself—to observe his environment, notice the dangers, and plan a safe course with the help of others. We cannot be with our children every minute as they grow to maturity, but we can do much to help them fend for themselves by preparing their hearts to follow Jesus.

The faith of each generation of believers must be fresh, vibrant, and personal. That is the only way to pass on the faith. If we fail in that, we become careless; and it is the careless who are crushed.

Oh, happy is the man who hears
Instruction's warning voice,
And who celestial wisdom makes
His early, only choice.

—Michael Bruce

If Thou But Suffer God to Guide Thee

1. If thou but suf - fer God to guide thee, And hope in Him thru all thy ways,
2. What can these anx - ious cares a - vail thee, These nev - er ceas - ing moans and sighs?
3. On - ly be still, and wait His lei - sure In cheer - ful hope, with heart con - tent
4. Sing, pray, and keep His ways un - swerv - ing, So do thine own part faith - ful - ly,
He'll give thee strength what - e'er be - tide thee, And bear thee thru the e - vil days;
What can it help, if thou be - wail thee O'er each dark mo - ment as it flies?
To take what - e'er thy Fa - ther's pleas - ure And all dis - cern - ing love hath sent;
And trust His Word– though un - de - serv - ing, Thou yet shalt find it true for thee;
Who trusts in God's un - chang - ing love Builds on the rock that naught can move.
Our cross and tri - als do but press The heav - ier for our bit - ter - ness.
Nor doubt our in - most wants are known To Him who chose us for His own.
God nev - er yet for - sook at need The soul that trust - ed Him in - deed.

WORDS BY GEORG NEUMARK (1641), TR. BY CATHERINE WINKWORTH (1863)
MUSIC BY GEORG NEUMARK (1641), ARR. BY JOHANN S. BACH (1723)

Wooing the Wrathful

READ:
Romans 12

A man that hath friends must shew himself friendly: and there is a friend that sticketh closer than a brother. —PROVERBS 18:24

The man and the woman named their new kitten Amiga, which means "friend." When Eliezer and Amiga met for the first time, Amiga was ready to establish a friendship. Eliezer, however, felt nothing but disdain and loathing for this intruder. He drew a deep breath and uttered an ominous snarl.

Amiga had experienced no unfriendliness, hatred, or fear in her short life. Wisely, she did not press the matter. But over the next week or two, she kept up a steady pressure of friendship. She refused to harbor a grudge. It was not long before Eliezer not only accepted her, but seemed genuinely fond of her. He willingly shared his cat food and even allowed her to play with his tail.

Abigail presents a greater challenge. She is reclusive and angry at the world. She appears from her wanderings once or twice a week. She refuses to let the other cats near her. A fierce growl rumbles spontaneously in her chest if any other feline trespasses into her personal space. Amiga is not deterred or even upset by Abigail's hostility. She seems to feel sure that eventually even this great antagonist will join her at the cat bowl.

This principle of sharing friendliness with everyone works just as well for us as it does for cats; in fact, it works better. The love of Christ can be magnified in us in a way Amiga will never experience. Is any antagonist so fierce that God's love cannot heal him of his anger when he turns to the Almighty in repentance? Restoration and goodwill are waiting for Abigail and the human sinner, whenever they are ready.

Light is stronger than darkness, warmth more powerful than cold;
Kindness will triumph o'er hatred; love may be righteous, yet bold.

Come, Ye Sinners

1. Come, ye sin - ners, poor and need - y, Weak and wound-ed, sick and sore,
2. Come, ye thirst - y, come and wel - come, God's free boun - ty glo - ri - fy
3. Come, ye wea - ry, heav - y lad - en, Bruised and bro - ken, full of sin;
Je - sus read - y stands to save you, Full of pit - y, love, and pow'r:
True be - lief and true re - pent - ance, Ev - 'ry grace that brings us nigh,
If you tar - ry, till you're bet - ter, You may nev - er en - ter in:
He is a - ble, He is a - ble, He is will - ing: doubt no more.
With - out mon - ey, with - out mon - ey; Come to Je - sus Christ and buy.
Not the right - eous, not the right - eous; Sin - ners Je - sus came to win.
He is a - ble, He is a - ble, He is will-ing: doubt no more.
With-out mon - ey, with - out mon - ey; Come to Je - sus Christ and buy.
Not the right - eous, not the right - eous; Sin - ners Je - sus came to win.

WORDS BY JOSEPH HART (1759)
MUSIC BY JEAN JACQUES ROUSSEAU (1750)

High Ground

READ:
Philippians 2:1–30

Let nothing be done through strife or vainglory; but in lowliness of mind let each esteem other better than themselves. —PHILIPPIANS 2:3

There are several reasons why Eliezer the cat likes cars. The roof of a car offers a smooth, comfortable, sun-warmed surface that is especially suitable for napping. From this height, he can monitor his surroundings even with his eyes mostly closed. The height gives him a feeling of safety, and resting is always easier when one feels safe. The elevated rooftop gives Eliezer a tactical advantage over any would-be adversaries. He can look down on anyone who approaches. Yes, cars are made for cats; about that he has no doubt.

Although people much prefer to be in their cars rather than on them, they tend to seek the high ground for much the same reasons cats do. People often strive with one another for an advantage. A high perch makes them feel safe. Looking down on others appeals to human nature.

Children may play "King of the Mountain" on a sand pile, but grownups are apt to play a more sophisticated version of the same game. A favorite ploy in this game is to introduce some criticism by mentioning that "people are talking." This puts the critic on the high ground, implying that he has the backing of others for his criticism. Of course he must be careful not to specify whom he heard talking or how many were involved; his position on the high ground will be much more secure if he lets the other person imagine the worst. This is but one of many ways people put others down to elevate themselves.

When Eliezer seeks the high ground, he is obeying his God-given instinct. God's Word shows people a better way.

Let thy grace, Lord, make me lowly,
Humble all my swelling pride;
Fallen, guilty, and unholy,
Greatness from mine eyes I'll hide.

—Unknown

Middle Ground*

READ:
Deuteronomy 30:10–20

I call heaven and earth to record this day against you, that I have set before you life and death, blessing and cursing: therefore choose life, that both thou and thy seed may live. —DEUTERONOMY 30:19

The mouse crouched under a loose board, perfectly still except for its wriggling nose and twitching whiskers. Eliezer the cat crouched equally motionless, mostly hidden behind a toolbox. His keen ears and his uplifted nose told him exactly where the mouse was. His haunches were coiled like springs, ready to launch in an instant. One misstep on the part of the mouse, and it would become his breakfast.

If the mouse had known cat language, he might have tried to work out a compromise with Eliezer. Would there not be benefit in living together in peace? He could ride on Eliezer's shoulders and scratch him behind the ears. Surely that would feel good to the big cat. The mouse could even keep a sharp lookout for fleas, snapping them up with his sharp little teeth. On the other hand, Eliezer's thick fur would keep the mouse warm.

However, Eliezer believed mice were to be eaten, and he was uncompromising on this point. No mouse had ever yet been able to talk him into letting it go. The cat was the mouse's enemy, and there was no middle ground between them.

Believers face an enemy far more formidable than the cat is to the mouse. Our enemy is uncompromising, vicious, and subtle. Far too many people have been seduced into seeking a middle ground with Satan. He tries to appear accommodating, but in truth, he desires nothing more than their eternal destruction.

There is no middle ground between God and Satan. One can never live in harmony with both. To seek a middle ground is to be estranged from God and within the grasp of Satan; and no one has ever yet talked Satan into releasing his catch.

There are two ways in this our day, one narrow and the other wide;
Who follows now the narrow way, will be despised on every side.

—adapted from the *Ausbund*

*Middle ground is a compromise between two extremes.

Common Ground*

READ:
Acts 17:16–31

. . . And hath made of one blood all nations of men for to dwell on all the face of the earth . . . —ACTS 17:26

Pepper is a dog, and Amiga is a cat. Pepper wags his tail and dances on his back legs; Amiga arches her back and rubs her head against the man's leg. Pepper barks and tells the world what he knows; Amiga purrs and keeps her thoughts to herself. We are not surprised by these differences. One is, after all, canine, while the other is feline, and they each act the way God created them to behave.

However, in spite of their differences, Pepper and Amiga have found areas of common interest. They share the same sunny spot on a cold winter day. They relish food from the same bowl on the back porch, and they both enjoy being scratched behind the ears.

People who enjoy interacting with other people look for areas of common interest. That is why many conversations open with a discussion of weather—sunshine and clouds, rain and snow, heat and cold affect us all. Farmers discuss crops, outdoorsmen swap hunting stories, and seamstresses compare fabrics.

The most important common ground anyone can have with another person is a love for the Lord. It is a beautiful thing to see two or more believers with their Bibles open, discussing the Word of God. How many opportunities to share this rich blessing slip by us while we discuss weather with a stranger, neglecting to steer the conversation toward spiritual realities. Let us actively seek out this area of mutual interest. Let us bask in it and relish it. It is a joy that Pepper and Amiga will never know.

Blest be the tie that binds
Our hearts in Christian love:
The fellowship of kindred minds
Is like to that above.

—John Fawcett

*Common ground may be defined as "an area of overlapping interest."

Blest Be the Tie That Binds

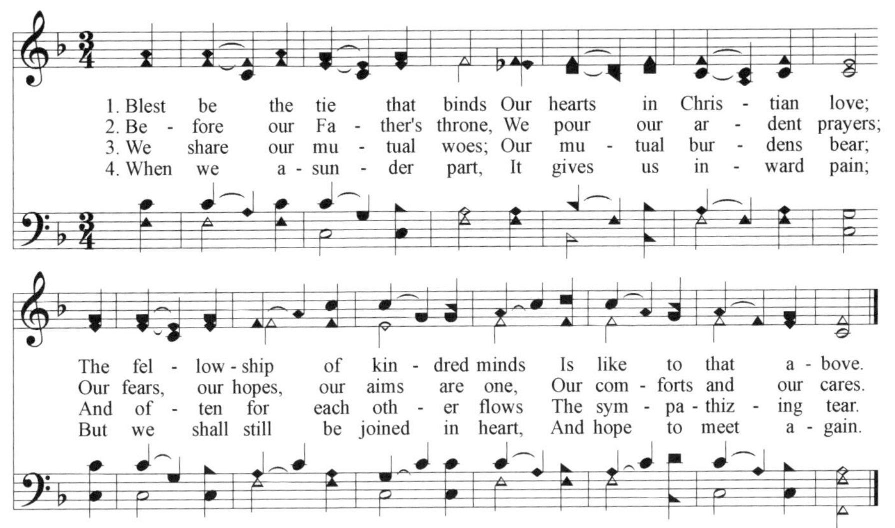

1. Blest be the tie that binds Our hearts in Chris - tian love;
2. Be - fore our Fa - ther's throne, We pour our ar - dent prayers;
3. We share our mu - tual woes; Our mu - tual bur - dens bear;
4. When we a - sun - der part, It gives us in - ward pain;
The fel - low - ship of kin - dred minds Is like to that a - bove.
Our fears, our hopes, our aims are one, Our com - forts and our cares.
And of - ten for each oth - er flows The sym - pa - thiz - ing tear.
But we shall still be joined in heart, And hope to meet a - gain.

WORDS BY JOHN FAWCETT
MUSIC BY HANS G. NAEGELI

In from the Cold

READ:
Mark 2:1–17

When Jesus heard it, he saith unto them, They that are whole have no need of the physician, but they that are sick: I came not to call the righteous, but sinners to repentance. —MARK 2:17

The night was windy, and a freezing rain slanted down. Pepper, Eliezer, and Amiga snuggled on the back porch. Pepper chewed a bone while Amiga played with Eliezer's tail. Abigail crouched under a bush in the backyard. Wet, cold, hungry, and angry, she was miserable inside and out. How she despised the pets on the porch. A savage growl rumbled in her chest. She riveted her gaze on the cat dish. She must have food. She needed it now.

As she approached, Eliezer stood and fixed her with an icy stare. *We don't need you here*, he seemed to say. *We're content and we all love each other. We don't need a smelly, irritable cat messing up our warm camaraderie.* And with that he drove her off into the night.

It was all so unnecessary. There was plenty of room on the porch and lots of food in the dish. Four companionable bodies would have generated more warmth than three. No one needed to be out in the cold on such a night. So who was to blame?

A group of believers enjoy their cozy church fellowship. A troubled teen from the community comes to church. Unkempt and disheveled, he slouches sullenly on the back bench. Those seated nearby notice an unpleasant odor and slide a bit farther down the bench. Many shudder at the thought of such a wretch messing up their cozy brotherhood. The youth may not look the part, but he is a sensitive person. He ducks out the back door as the pastor pronounces the benediction. He will remain in a cold, dangerous world, unprepared to meet his Maker, and who is to blame?

Christ promised to make believers fishers of men, and they do not fish exclusively for sinners who smell good.

Our call is to seek out the souls of men,
But if they are ugly and mean, what then?

Rescue the Perishing

Chorus
1. Res - cue the per - ish - ing, Care for the dy - ing, Snatch them in pit - y from sin and the grave; Weep o'er the err - ing one, Lift up the fall - en, Tell them of Je - sus, the Might - y to save.
2. Down in the hu - man heart, Crushed by the tempt - er, Feel - ings lie bur - ied that grace can re - store; Touched by a lov - ing hand, Wak - ened by kind - ness, Chords that were bro - ken will vi - brate once more.
3. Res - cue the per - ish - ing, Du - ty de - mands it; Strength for thy la - bor the Lord will pro - vide; Back to the nar - row way Pa - tient - ly win them; Tell the poor wan - d'rer a Sav - ior has died.
Res - cue the per - ish - ing, Care for the dy - ing; Je - sus is mer - ci - ful, Je - sus will save.

WORDS BY FANNY J. CROSBY
MUSIC BY WILLIAM H. DOANE

Pepper's Philosophy

READD:
Esther 3

I wrote unto the church: but Diotrephes, who loveth to have the preeminence among them, receiveth us not. —3 JOHN 1:9

Pepper is a fat little Chihuahua. As with humans, his priorities grow out of his philosophy of life. Pepper's philosophy is so simple it can be stated in two short words: ME FIRST. He has worked out his philosophy in two simple mealtime rules that all the cats understand: first, Pepper gets the biggest and tastiest portion of any food served, and second, as soon as Pepper has wolfed down his choice morsel, anything the cats have not yet consumed is his too.

One day the man gave the pets a few bits of grilled steak left over from the day before. As soon as Pepper's keen nose identified the gift for the rarity it was, it was clear to him that this food was much too fine to be wasted on cats. When the man tossed Pepper his piece, he swallowed it with unbelievable speed, not bothering to chew it or taste it. The resulting fit of choking, wheezing, and coughing did not deter him from trying to intercept the pieces being thrown to the cats.

Why didn't Pepper take his piece of meat off to a secluded corner? There he could have lain down and held the delicacy between his paws as he nibbled and savored it, his keen nose bringing him sensory pleasure beyond anything humans can experience. No, Pepper's philosophy prevents such a positive response to the gift he has received. Once again, Pepper has been defeated by his own selfish philosophy.

What governs our priorities as humans? Do we do all for the glory of God? Do we care deeply for others, or do we share Pepper's philosophy? No matter what answer we give, our actions will reveal the truth.

If I must be first, my plight is the worst.

None of Self and All of Thee

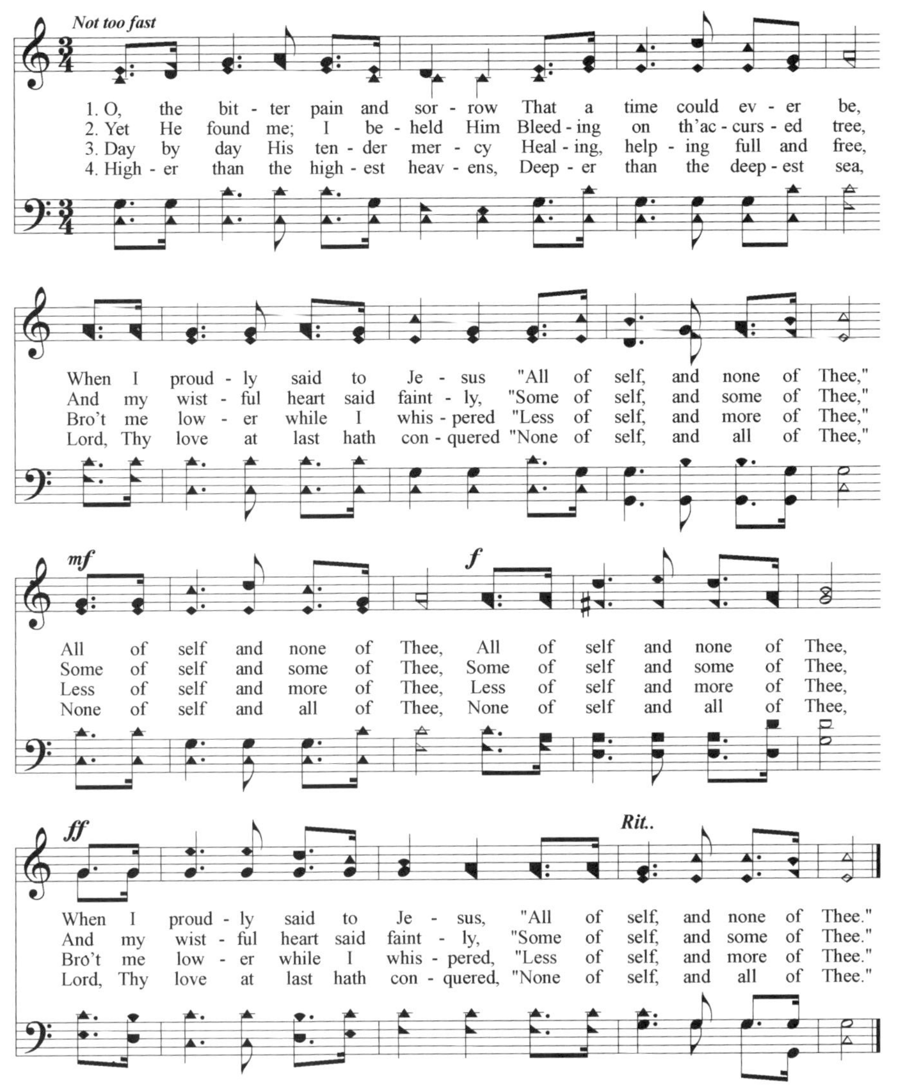
Not too fast
1. O, the bit - ter pain and sor - row That a time could ev - er be,
2. Yet He found me; I be - held Him Bleed - ing on th'ac - curs - ed tree,
3. Day by day His ten - der mer - cy Heal - ing, help - ing full and free,
4. High - er than the high - est heav - ens, Deep - er than the deep - est sea,
When I proud - ly said to Je - sus "All of self, and none of Thee,"
And my wist - ful heart said faint - ly, "Some of self, and some of Thee,"
Bro't me low - er while I whis - pered "Less of self, and more of Thee,"
Lord, Thy love at last hath con - quered "None of self, and all of Thee,"
mf
All of self and none of Thee, All of self and none of Thee,
Some of self and some of Thee, Some of self and some of Thee,
Less of self and more of Thee, Less of self and more of Thee,
None of self and all of Thee, None of self and all of Thee,
f
ff
When I proud - ly said to Je - sus, "All of self, and none of Thee."
And my wist - ful heart said faint - ly, "Some of self, and some of Thee."
Bro't me low - er while I whis - pered, "Less of self, and more of Thee."
Lord, Thy love at last hath con - quered, "None of self, and all of Thee."
Rit..

Words by Theodore Monod
Music by James McGranahan

Pepper's Dilemma

READ:
1 Samuel 17:2–31

The liberal soul shall be made fat: and he that watereth shall be watered also himself. —PROVERBS 11:25

The meat was clearly visible inside the wire mesh box. The man had baited the box trap to be set out later, but for now it sat beside the back porch. The cats set to work seeing how they might get to the meat. They poked their paws through the wire, trying one angle and another, all to no avail. The trap door was shut, and there was no way to get the meat.

Pepper, the fat little Chihuahua, arrived on the scene, woofed away the cats, and tried his paw at securing the prize. But with his short legs, he had even less chance of success than the cats did.

It was cold, and soon Pepper was shivering and ready to return to his rug in the garage. But what if one of the cats figured out how to get that meat in his absence? He rushed at the cats, driving them away from the trap, but every time he started for his comfortable mat, they came sneaking back. He would have to choose whether to stay outside in the cold to guard "his" meat or to risk letting the cats get it while he slumbered. What a dilemma!

Sometimes we get into similar dilemmas. Like Pepper's, ours are self-inflicted. If we were just a bit more sharing and a bit less defensive, life would go much more smoothly for us and those around us. Pepper would be happier, healthier, and more relaxed if he would freely share his food with the cats. We have many more opportunities to share than Pepper does, and we can have godly love and concern for others. That is something Pepper will never understand.

Serving self is mighty hard work,
For self is a slave driver cruel;
With self as your master, you never may shirk,
And your pay will be that of a fool.

The Profile of a Hypocrite

READ: Romans 2:1–16

Therefore thou art inexcusable, O man, whosoever thou art that judgest: for wherein thou judgest another, thou condemnest thyself; for thou that judgest doest the same things. —ROMANS 2:1

It was the darkest hour of the night when the neighbor's big black dog made his way to the man's back porch in search of food. So well did he blend with the darkness that he seemed to materialize from nowhere. He followed his nose to the cat's dish and began helping himself.

Inside the man's house, a hand flicked a light switch and flooded the porch with light. Startled, the dog whirled with a growl and vanished into the night.

A few days later, a kite went astray and landed on the neighbor's property. Knowing his neighbor as a congenial person, the man crossed onto the other farm in search of the wayward kite.

"Ruff, ruff—bow, wow wow!" roared a canine voice filled with righteous indignation. There was nothing furtive now about the handsome black dog bounding to intercept the trespasser. "What are you doing on my master's farm?" he seemed to demand. "You don't belong here; go home and stay there."

As the man carried the kite back to his side of the property line, he was reflective. Something in the manner of his neighbor's dog reminded him of a dark human heart, a heart with secrets it prefers not to expose to the light. Whenever some hand turns the light of God's Word on his darkness, he runs for cover. Yet strangely, this same person is eager to expose the shortcomings of others.

The incongruity of such behavior is lost on the dog, but thoughtful Christians will recognize such inconsistencies in their own hearts and welcome the Holy Spirit to point His divine light where it is needed. What that light reveals will keep one too busy to be critical of others.

Accusation's tongue directed at another person's fault may obscure that the accuser is not doing what he ought.

Remember to Look Up

READ:
Joshua 7

Behold, the judge standeth before the door. —JAMES 5:9

The yellow tomcat crouched in the weeds along the edge of the man's property as the twilight deepened. The only evidence of his growing impatience was the twitching tip of his long tail. When he deemed it sufficiently dark and quiet, he began moving stealthily toward the back porch and the cat dish. With every sense alert for danger, he eased onto the back porch. He paused once more. Probing the darkness with his eyes and ears, he looked in every direction—but one.

Satisfied that all was well, the tomcat began to crunch cat food. He did not know the man stood just inside the closed door, looking down at him through the window. Every few moments he stopped crunching to look and listen, but he never thought to look up, and so he never saw the man, who would one day hold him responsible for his nighttime forays.

Many sins are committed in private. A closed door, a darkened environment, a cell phone, an Internet connection, no one else around—these may make a person feel safe. He looks in every direction except one. He is alone, he thinks—no one will ever know.

A youth travels alone. A motel beckons. Television, a late-night movie, or worse wait beyond the closed door. No one knows he is here. But is he sure he is alone? Does he remember to look up?

Someone is watching who will eventually hold him responsible for his nighttime forays. "Behold, the judge standeth before the door."

The Judge's eyes all sins behold,
And all dark secrets will unfold.

Prepare to Meet Thy God

1. Care-less soul, why will you lin - ger, Wand-'ring from the fold of God?
2. Why so tho't-less are you stand - ing While the fleet - ing years go by,
3. If you spurn the in - vi - ta - tion Till the Spir - it shall de - part,
Hear you not the in - vi - ta - tion? O pre - pare to meet thy God.
And your life is spent in fol - ly? O pre - pare to meet thy God.
Then you'll see your sad con - di - tion, Un - pre - pared to meet thy God.
Chorus
Care - less soul, O heed the warn-ing, For your
O care - less soul, heed the warn - ing,
life will soon be gone; O how sad to
will soon be gone, O yes your life will soon be gone; to face the judg-ment
face the judg-ment, Un-pre-pared to meet thy God.
O how sad to face the judg - ment, Un - pre - pared to meet thy God.

WORDS AND MUSIC BY J. H. STANLEY

The Harshness of Love

READ: Revelation 19:11–21

He, that being often reproved hardeneth his neck, shall suddenly be destroyed, and that without remedy. —PROVERBS 29:1

The man enjoyed animal pets, especially cats; and he disliked weapons, especially highpowered guns. So why was he padding on stealthy feet across his back deck at 4 a.m., clutching a shotgun?

A yellow, battle-scarred tom had been terrorizing Eliezer and the man's other cats for weeks. The big cat seemed to appear from nowhere, leaping from the shadows and raking his victims with teeth and claws until they screamed for mercy. The wily creature made a mockery of the man's most cunning attempts to stop him. So at last it had come to this.

We serve a God who is kind and good to all creation, especially to people, and who is unwilling that any should perish. So why do we read in the Bible of a place of eternal torment for those who refuse to serve God in life?

God is love. He loves us so much that He gave His only Son to die so that we might have eternal life. But pure love is also just. God not only saves us but also calls us and empowers us to holy living. His justice will not allow evil to defy His holiness. If God did not love His people, He might shrug and say, "Who cares? So what if a little sin slips in here and there to taint the purity of Christ's bride?"

Because God is holy, heaven awaits His holy people. Because God is just, hell awaits the unrepentant sinner. Because God is love, He is uncompromising—yes, even harsh against anything that threatens His beloved. The man's efforts to safeguard his cats are puny when compared to the outpouring of the holy wrath of an almighty God against evil.

The day of wrath, that dreadful day,
When heav'n and earth shall pass away!
What pow'rs shall be the sinner's stay?
How shall he meet that dreadful day?

—Thomas of Celano (#570 in *The Christian Hymnary*)

The Skill of Listening

READ:
Nehemiah 8

Hear counsel, and receive instruction, that thou mayest be wise in thy latter end. —PROVERBS 19:20

Before Amiga the cat leaves the safety of the back porch at night, she listens with all her being to what is going on around her. She swivels and adjusts her ears to screen out distracting sounds. She turns her head this way and that. When she thinks she hears something of special interest, her focus intensifies. Her ears go fully forward and she faces the direction from which the noise came.

While all this is going on, she maintains perfect silence, not purring, not meowing, and certainly not barking. She does not engage in any other activity while she listens. She does not groom her fur or scratch her ear. All her attention is focused on listening. By the time she steps off the porch, she knows what is out there. No enemy will surprise her. She has done her porch work.

Pepper the dog has keen ears as well, and he also knows how to use them. However, he has one compulsion Amiga does not share—he feels compelled to tell the world what he hears or thinks he hears. Amiga reveals none of the information she has gathered by listening, leaving her observers to wonder what she knows.

I would hate to challenge either of my pets to a listening contest. I have a number of bad habits that interfere with my listening. Sometimes I am not really interested in what I am being told. Sometimes I begin formulating my response while I should still be listening. I also tend to lack focus. At times I have preconceived ideas that interfere with hearing what others say. So many bad habits! My dog and cat have much to teach me, if only I will observe and listen.

When hearts are crushed and teardrops glisten,
Oh, be not rushed, but stop and listen.

What Amiga Cannot See

READ: Genesis 1

In the beginning God created the heaven and the earth. —GENESIS 1:1

Sometimes I wish I could see as well as Amiga the cat. I don't know for sure how much she sees, but she seems able to see in the dark, and that gives her a big advantage over me. Imagine having no need for reading lights, night lights, street lights, flashlights, security lights, or headlights! Yet there are some things to which Amiga seems blind.

I have never seen Amiga gazing in awe at the golden splendor of a setting sun, nor does she seem entranced by silver stars or a full moon. She walks right past the flower bed, never pausing to admire the delicate petals of the budding roses. She does not notice whether the lawn is mowed and trimmed or the trellis freshly painted. She *does* take a keen interest in the birds at my backyard feeder, but I do not get the impression that she is admiring their brilliant plumage or marveling at their effortless flight. No, her gaze seems calculating—even savage.

God has given us humans a special ability to enjoy the beauty of our surroundings. We notice shades in color, symmetry in design, order in arrangements, and delicacy in perfection. Believers enjoy yet another dimension of sight. We see the omnipotent hand of an artistic God in all of nature. We can lift our hearts to the Creator in praise for the wonders we behold on every side—and I wouldn't trade that privilege for the best night vision in the world.

Why should the wonders He hath wrought, be lost in silence and forgot?

—Isaac Watts

Can You Count the Stars?

1. Can you count the stars of eve - ning That are shin - ning in the sky?
2. Can you count the birds that war - ble In the sun - shine all the day?
3. Can you count the man - y chil - dren In their lit - tle beds at night,
Can you count the clouds that dai - ly O - ver all the world go by?
Can you count the lit - tle fish - es That in sparkl - ing wa - ters play?
Who with - out a tho't of sor - row Rise a - gain at morn - ing light?
God, the Lord, who doth not slum - ber, Keep - eth all the bound-less num - ber:
God the Lord, their num - ber know - eth, For each one His care He show - eth:
God the Lord, who dwells in heav - en, Lov - ing care to each has giv - en:
But He car - eth more for thee, But He car - eth more for thee.
Shall He not re - mem - ber thee? Shall He not re - mem - ber thee?
He has not for - got - ten thee, He has not for - got - ten thee.

Words by Johann Hey
Music: German Folk Tune

The Language of Barking

READ: Acts 19:23–41

Wherefore, my beloved brethren, let every man be swift to hear, slow to speak, slow to wrath. —JAMES 1:19

For many years I have enjoyed studying words and language. I have had scant success in learning Pennsylvania German, but I do know a little Spanish as a second language. Lately I have been studying the language of barking, not to speak it, but to understand it better. Pepper, our Chihuahua, is my tutor.

Barking is a language that demands attention. It is usually initiated before all the facts are in, and it tends to intensify as more facts come to light. Barkers don't always know what they are barking about; they may bark just because someone else barked. Some barkers seem to bark because they like hearing themselves bark. Barkers speak in loud, abrupt bursts of sound that usually mean nothing friendly.

The underlying philosophy of barking is that the barker first establishes in his mind what is normal for his surroundings; after that, anything that invades that normal space—any noise, movement, smell, or sight that does not belong—must be barked at. The more threatening the intrusion, the more intense the barking. Large barkers have a ring of authority in their barking. Small barkers like Pepper sound shriller and often add extra behaviors for impact, such as jerking the whole body with each bark and kicking up tufts of grass with stiff legs.

Barking is usually done by dogs. As I said, I am not interested in speaking this language; yet as I review the paragraphs above, I have the uneasy feeling that I may be more proficient in this language than I realized.

Understanding—shallow, dark—
Does not make barkers cease to bark;
And that perception lacks connection,
Does not deter this predilection.

The Language of Sniffing

READ:
Acts 9

Dead flies cause the ointment of the apothecary to send forth a stinking savour: so doth a little folly him that is in reputation for wisdom and honour. —ECCLESIASTES 10:1

Eliezer the cat is quite skilled in the language of sniffing. Lifting his keen nose into the air will tell him if the neighbor's big black dog is upwind, and holding it close to the concrete floor will tell him if the marauding tom has recently visited the food dish on the back porch. Pepper the dog is even more adept at this language. At a rapid trot, with his nose in the grass, he can work out last night's zigzag trail of a visiting opossum.

Humans use this language with varying degrees of proficiency. Sniffing can be either constructive or destructive, depending on the sniffer's purpose. The language of sniffing is indirect; the sniffer must be able to collect and interpret clues that lead him to the information he seeks. Some people resort to the language of sniffing to gather unsavory information about others in order to support a gossip habit. They become skilled at assembling scattered bits of information into a story, using imagination and speculation to fill in the gaps. The language of sniffing, used in this manner, becomes extremely destructive.

Others utilize sniffing in a beneficial way. These tend to be quiet, sensitive individuals. Though they are very observant, they never gossip about their conclusions. These people are able to sniff out the discouraged and give them a sunny smile or an encouraging word. They sniff out the weary and the overworked, to whom they lend a helping hand. They sniff out the disillusioned and the misguided and share prayer or a few words of counsel.

As long as the world stands, dogs and cats will sniff footprints and gossipers will ply their malicious trade, but there will always be a need for more people to exercise the language of sniffing in a constructive way.

As you gather the clues of facts that exist,
The urge to gossip steadfastly resist.

The Language of Growling

READ: 1 Samuel 20:24–34

And the servant of the Lord must not strive; but be gentle unto all men, apt to teach, patient. —2 TIMOTHY 2:24

Growling is a language associated with dogs and cats, though animals such as raccoons and opossums speak the language as well. Growling is a universally understood language.

Growling sends a warning. The growler is not happy with what is going on, and he may be thinking of going on the offensive. Growlers are unfriendly and not usually in a mood to work the situation out peacefully.

Growling may be short or long. The longer the growling goes on, the less likely it is that the growler will take further action. On the other hand, a short, fierce growl may signal that someone needs to comply immediately or face dire consequences.

Some people have in their homes a secluded and quiet room called a den, suitable for reading, writing, and relaxation. One little boy asked his friend, "Does your house have a den?" The other replied, "No, my daddy just growls all over the house." Sad to say, some people do speak this language, and worse still, dads seem more prone to growling than anyone else.

Does the Bible have anything to say about people who growl? Yes, it certainly does. Today's key verse leaves no room in the vocabulary of God's children for the language of growling. Dads need to be firm sometimes; they may even need to warn of dire consequences if someone's behavior doesn't change, but this signal should not be sent by growling. God has given us the ability to say anything that needs to be said in a sanctified manner. Growling should be left to the animal kingdom.

My thoughts before they are my own
Are to my God distinctly known;
He knows the words I mean to speak,
Ere from my opening lips they break.

—Isaac Watts (#106 in *The Christian Hymnary*)

Angry Words

1. An - gry words! O let them nev - er From the tongue un - bri - dled slip;
2. Love is much too pure and ho - ly, Friend - ship is too sa - cred far,
3. Let our words be sweet - ly spo - ken, Let kind tho'ts be great - ly stirred;
May the heart's best im - pulse ev - er Check them ere they soil the lip.
For a mo - ment's reck - less fol - ly Thus to des - o - late and mar.
Show our love to one an - oth - er With a - bun - dance of kind words.
Chorus
"Love one an - oth - er," thus saith the Sav - ior; Chil - dren o -
Love each oth - er, love each oth - er,
bey the Fa - ther's blest com - mand. "Love one an - oth - er," thus saith the
'tis the Fa - ther's blest com - mand. Love each oth - er,
Sav - ior; Chil - dren o - bey His blest com - mand.
love each oth - er, 'tis His blest com - mand.
3
3
3
3
3
3
3

WORDS: SUNDAY SCHOOL TEACHER, ST. 3 BY BETTY BENDER
MUSIC BY H. R. PALMER / ARRANGEMENT BY WILL W. SLATER

The Language of Purring

READ: 2 Corinthians 1

Wherefore comfort yourselves together, and edify one another, even as also ye do. —1 THESSALONIANS 5:11

The warble of a songbird on a spring morning inspires us, and the chorus of tree frogs on a summer night refreshes us. The whimper of a puppy touches us, and the scream of a stallion thrills us. But I can't think of any sound in the animal kingdom more comforting than the sound of a cat purring. A cat's purr is a genuine expression of pleasure and contentment. No cat will pretend to be at peace when it is not—there is no fake purr. It is this quality of genuineness that makes purring a comforting sound.

Although people do not purr, they do comfort each other; but not all forms of comfort are equal. A friend we'll call George was diagnosed with cancer. His worldly buddies came by, slapped him on the back, and wished him luck. A godly man spoke with George one day and encouraged him to seek the Lord. The man said he would pray for him. George's worldly buddies left him feeling hollow and empty, but he found deep comfort in the words of his godly friend.

Today's Bible reading explains that we are comforted by the God of all comfort. In turn, after we ourselves are comforted, we can comfort others by sharing that deep, rich comfort which comes from God. People who do not know and love God do not know how to give meaningful comfort. They have to make do with a slap on the back and a "good luck" wish. I am thankful that as a child of God I can experience the full, sweet comfort that comes from the Holy Spirit and fellow believers.

No, people don't purr—but then again, maybe some do.

Comfort best comes from the sureness of hope,
A lifeline for those at the end of their rope.

Wonderful Words of Life

Chorus
1. Sing them o - ver a - gain to me, Won - der - ful words of Life;
2. Christ, the bless - ed One, gives to all, Won - der - ful words of Life;
3. Sweet - ly ech - o the gos - pel call, Won - der - ful words of Life;
Let me more of their beau - ty see, Won - der - ful words of Life.
Sin - ner, list to the lov - ing call, Won - der - ful words of Life.
Of - fer par - don and peace to all, Won - der - ful words of Life.
Words of life and beau - ty, Teach me faith and du - ty;
All so free - ly giv - en, Woo - ing us to heav - en;
Je - sus, on - ly Sav - ior, Sanc - ti - fy for - ev - er;
Beau - ti - ful words, won - der - ful words, Won - der - ful words of Life;
Beau - ti - ful words, won - der - ful words, Won - der - ful words of Life.

WORDS AND MUSIC BY PHILLIP P. BLISS

OTHER ANIMALS, BIRDS & INSECTS

Invaders

READ:
Acts 5:1–16

Some men's sins are open beforehand, going before to judgment; and some men they follow after. —1 TIMOTHY 5:24

The siding under the garage window was beginning to sag. Some exploratory prodding revealed that the wall behind the siding was spongy and weak. The next Saturday morning we began removing the siding from the garage wall to uncover the problem. It soon became apparent that rainwater had been finding its way into the wall structure for a long time. The studs and plywood sheathing were moist and rotted.

As we dug deeper, we discovered insect tunnels in the wood, and then we saw the pale, marching termites that had made them. Soon there was a gaping hole in the wall and a nearby pile of insulation and decomposed wood exposed for all to see. Later, after much hard work, it was a great relief to finally have firm new studs nailed back in place, covered by fresh plywood.

The termite is not the only menace that does its destructive work out of sight. Hypocrisy likes to hide itself behind the veneer of good deeds, church attendance, and fine talk. Ill will is concealed behind a sweet smile, lust is confined to the innermost thoughts, hateful gossip presents itself as heartfelt concern, and pride poses as deep humility.

However, like the termite, sin cannot remain hidden: sooner or later, it will lie exposed like a pile of decayed rubbish for all to see. The Bible says, "He that covereth his sins shall not prosper: but whoso confesseth and forsaketh them shall have mercy" (Proverbs 28:13). Confessing our sins is like tearing rotted wood out of a wall. It is an unpleasant task, but corruption must be removed before integrity can be restored. What a blessed relief to experience forgiveness and renewal!

Hidden sin the heart will harden;
Jesus Christ alone can pardon.

Food Chain

READ:
Luke 9:1–17

And the things that thou hast heard of me among many witnesses, the same commit thou to faithful men, who shall be able to teach others also. —2 TIMOTHY 2:2

Nature survives by means of a food chain: the frog eats the fly, the snake eats the frog, the hawk eats the snake, and so on. In each case, the life of the weaker is sacrificed so that the stronger may live. Nature's food chain is a saga of victim and victor, a sequence of suffering and satisfaction, a cycle of death and life.

Each link of the food chain is marked not only by a loss of life, but also by a loss of efficiency. Ecologists estimate that it takes 762 pounds of forage to produce 59 pounds of moose to produce one pound of wolf.* Survival in the wild is punctuated by pain and loss.

To nourish our souls, God has designed a much better food chain. This food chain is characterized by renewed life and blessing rather than by loss of life and inefficiency. The New Testament gives us a glimpse of this food chain in action. We read that Timothy's grandmother Lois and his mother Eunice transmitted their unfeigned faith to Timothy. The spiritual well-being of each family member was enhanced not only by receiving, but also by giving.

When Jesus fed the multitude, He broke bread and gave to His disciples, who in turn distributed to the crowd. It is our sacred privilege to share with others what we have received of the Lord. In this way we form the links of a food chain that abounds with blessing and provision.

When nature preys, the victim pays.
The Christian prays to share God's ways.

* "Ecology," *World Book Encyclopedia*, 1994, vol. 6, p. 53–56.

How to Take a Dust Bath

READ:
James 3:1–18

Let us draw near with a true heart in full assurance of faith, having our hearts sprinkled from an evil conscience, and our bodies washed with pure water. —HEBREWS 10:22

Prince Rooster and his hens enjoy taking dust baths. They find a dry, dusty spot and scratch out a little depression. They flatten themselves in the dirt, fluffing out their feathers and wriggling this way and that. They work their feet to throw the dust up over their backs. By all appearances, this feels very good to them; but not even Prince Rooster has found a way to look dignified while taking a dust bath. No matter how he does it, he is still wallowing in the dirt.

People do not wallow in the dirt. We greatly prefer to clean ourselves in warm, sudsy water. Yet on second thought, maybe we are not as clean as we imagine. Many people enjoy the muck and filth on the Internet, television, and in newspapers. Gossipers like nothing better than a good dust bath on the telephone. They fluff their self-righteous feathers and kick up the dust with their feet, which are "swift in running to mischief."

But none of *us* would do that—of course not. We might occasionally share a concern that requires us to reveal some unsavory (or savory?) details, but we wouldn't think of gossiping. Yet the image of Prince Rooster wriggling in the dust keeps coming to mind. As we ponder the matter, we should be aware of an important difference between the dust baths Prince Rooster takes and the ones people take: chickens probably find some benefit in kicking up dust, but our dirt baths always harm ourselves and usually injure others as well. Today's theme verse provides warm sudsy water with which to cleanse ourselves daily.

Stay out of dust, avoid the dirt;
Don't think or say the things that hurt.

King Rooster

READ:
Proverbs 16:1–19

Only by pride cometh contention: but with the well advised is wisdom.
—PROVERBS 13:10

King Rooster was a handsome fellow. His red-brown plumage glistened in the morning sunlight, and his flaming comb crowned a bobbing head. His gold-rimmed eyes peered intensely this way and that as he strutted about his enclosure. His crowing dominated the peaceful morning. He was the finest rooster in his little universe.

The next moment a door opened, and a woman carrying chicken feed stepped into his space. Puffing his feathers, King Rooster immediately attacked the intruder. Wise in the ways of roosters, the woman fended him off and filled his feeder, but his attack reminded her of the succulent taste of fried chicken. She left the enclosure, and King Rooster pecked hungrily at the food, unaware that his cocky actions had shortened his life expectancy.

Here are some lessons we can learn from King Rooster:

- Self-importance hinders our usefulness for God.
- Any attractiveness or ability we have is given by God for His glory and is no credit to us.
- The universe is much larger than our little world.
- Crowing disturbs the peace.
- We are not nearly as important or indispensable as we may think.
- We should not attack others.
- Those we view as a threat may be trying to help us.
- Pride brings unrest and trouble.
- Ill-considered actions may shorten our life of service for God.

Our feet are for serving, not strutting. Our hearts are for pondering, not puffing. Our heads are for bowing, not bobbing. A wise old minister used to say, "It's always a good time to be humble."

O Master, let me walk with thee
In lowly paths of service free.

—Washington Gladd

O Master, Let Me Walk with Thee

1. O Mas - ter let me walk with Thee In low - ly paths of ser - vice free;
2. Help me the slow of heart to move By some clear, win - ning word of love;
3. Teach me Thy pa - tience! Still with Thee In clos - er, dear - er com - pa - ny,
4. In hope that sends a shin - ing ray Far down the fu - ture's broad - 'ning way,
Tell me Thy se - cret; help me bear The strain of toil, the fret of care.
Teach me the way - ward feet to stay, And guide them in the home - ward way.
In work that keeps faith sweet and strong, In trust that tri - umphs o - ver wrong.
In peace that on - ly Thou canst give, With Thee, O Mas - ter, let me live.

WORDS BY W. GLADDEN
MUSIC BY H. P. SMITH

The Man and the Mosquito

READ: Hebrews 9

For if the blood of bulls and of goats, and the ashes of an heifer sprinkling the unclean, sanctifieth to the purifying of the flesh: how much more shall the blood of Christ . . . purge your conscience from dead works to serve the living God? —HEBREWS 9:13–14

The mosquito was famished, and she craved blood. She needed blood for the eggs she would lay, so there could be more mosquitoes, but first she must have warm, life-giving blood.

Then she smelled the man. Ah! Here was blood and to spare—rivers of delicious, throbbing blood. She closed in on her target, the high-pitched whine of her wings joining the hum of dozens of her sisters.

The man slapped himself and waved his arms. The thought of wasting his precious blood on one of these creatures that would use it to propagate more of her irksome kind was irritating. If she escaped his vengeful hand, she would gorge and then fly off, leaving behind an itchy welt and maybe a disease.

Later, within the shelter of his workplace, the man grew thoughtful. Although the mosquito desperately wanted it, she could not properly value the man's precious blood. Does not mankind have the same tendency toward the blood of Jesus? At a fathomless cost, Jesus offered His precious, life-giving blood to redeem humans from their wretched, sinful condition. Although they know they need it, many people trample it carelessly underfoot, scorning the costly provision for their own salvation.

Surely, the greatest insult to the blood of Jesus is when a hypocrite professes Christianity falsely, using it as a cloak to cover a secret, ungodly life. But God will not be mocked. The life-giving blood of Christ serves only to cleanse the sins of the genuine seeker. And at the judgment, God will surely expose all hypocrisy.

What a wonderful, wonderful Saviour,
Who would die on the cross for me!
Freely shedding His precious lifeblood,
That the sinner might be made free.

—F. A. Graves

I Gave My Life for Thee

1. I gave My life for thee, My precious blood I shed,
2. My Fa - ther's house of light, My glo - ry - cir - cled throne,
3. I suf - fered much for thee, More than thy tongue can tell,
4. And I have bro't to thee, Down from My home a - bove,
That thou might'st ran - som be, And quick - ened from the dead;
I left for earth - ly night, For wan - d'rings sad and lone;
Of bit - t'rest ag - o - ny, To res - cue thee from hell;
Sal - va - tion full and free, My par - don and My love;
Chorus
I gave, I gave My life for thee: What hast thou giv - en for Me?
I left, I left it all for thee: Hast thou left aught for Me?
I've borne, I've borne it all for thee: What hast thou borne for Me?
I bring, I bring rich gifts to thee: What hast thou bro't for Me?
I gave, I gave My life for thee: What hast thou giv - en for Me?
I left, I left it all for thee: Hast thou left aught for Me?
I've borne, I've borne it all for thee: What hast thou borne for Me?
I bring, I bring rich gifts to thee: What hast thou bro't for Me?

Words by Frances R. Havergal
Music by Phillip P. Bliss

Wee Winged Warriors

READ: 1 Samuel 25:2–25, 32–35

Be kindly affectioned one to another with brotherly love; in honour preferring one another. —ROMANS 12:10

A hummingbird feeder was suspended just outside the kitchen window by a wire. The feeder was an inverted plastic bottle filled with sugar water that emptied into a bright red dispenser with ten ports. It should have been possible for ten hummingbirds to drink at the same time, but this never happened. Though there were dozens of hungry birds, the hummers had never learned to share. They came to the feeder with two objectives: objective number two was to get a drink of sugar water, and objective number one was to make sure no one else got a drink. With fierce little squeaks they darted about, guarding access to the feeder.

Watching, the man wished he could line up all the hummingbirds on the clothesline and lecture them. He'd start by explaining how illogical and foolish their behavior was. Their aggressive behavior made for high stress and low satisfaction every day. But then he stopped in his tracks as he realized he was the one who should get in line first for a lecture. Wasn't it just last week that he'd resisted Joe's good idea for no other reason than that he hadn't thought of it first? And hadn't he recently refrained from giving his son a well-earned compliment because . . . well, why? What was it that made him want to be first, to have the biggest piece of pie, and to keep others quiet so he could talk?

The man bowed his head amid the chorus of angry hummingbird squeaks and prayed, "God, help me think more of others and less of myself."

Within our passioned hearts instill
The calm that endeth strain and strife;
Make us thy ministers of life;
Purge us from lusts that curse and kill!

—W. M. Vories

Takers and Givers

READ:
Matthew 10:1–16

And whosoever shall give to drink unto one of these little ones a cup of cold water only in the name of a disciple, verily I say unto you, he shall in no wise lose his reward. —MATTHEW 10:42

Visitors to our part of North Carolina are eagerly greeted, not only by their human friends, but by other creatures as well. In the spring, swarms of gnats are eager to meet the newcomer. These tiny insects perch on any available skin, leaving itchy red welts where they bite. Though they make no effort to avoid being killed, they overwhelm people by sheer numbers.

Deer flies greet guests in small groups. Shaped like fighter jets, they orbit one's head at bewildering speed. They land and take off again with such precise timing that their victims slap themselves an instant after the fly has darted away. While the person is distracted with the deer fly, a tick may be edging near. And everyone knows what the mosquito has in mind when they hear her high-pitched drone.

Although gnats, flies, ticks, and mosquitoes have different techniques, they all have one thing in common: they are parasites. The word *parasite* stems from the Greek words *para* (beside) and *sitos* (food). The word originated in ancient Greek and Roman culture, where the wealthy often had followers who would flatter, entertain, and dote on them in the interest of eating at their table. Today the word is used to describe people or creatures who always take but give nothing of value in return.

Jesus taught the doctrine of giving. Although He had nothing good to say about the wealthy who skimmed from their abundance to toss a few coins to the widows and orphans, He showed us that we all have much to share. Even the poorest can present the Gospel. We can offer comfort, bestow blessing, provide encouragement, and share inspiration. The parasite mentality says, "I'll take from another so I can live." The believer's motto is, "Freely I have received, freely I will give."

Since blessings we have each obtained,
Let generous hand be not refrained.

The Bee

READ:
Genesis 45:1–15, 50:15–20

For as the heavens are higher than the earth, so are my ways higher than your ways, and my thoughts than your thoughts. —ISAIAH 55:9

I was working in the garden shed one April morning. Rays of sunshine slanted through the clear glass of the roof window overhead. The door was open, and spring drifted in on fragrant wings. Suddenly the peace was shattered by a tiny roar. It was the distinct sound of a bumblebee. On almost any other morning, Mr. Bee would have stopped to chew a couple of holes in the wooden structure, but not this morning. He had places to go and things to do. However, as he dove through the door of the shed, his little bee eyes were instantly attracted to the lighted roof window above and the inviting blue sky beyond. At full throttle, he shot for the heavens.

He never saw it coming. He hit the glass full force. Pain exploded in his tiny brain. Most frustrating, he didn't know what he had hit. He could not discover what had arrested his rapid ascent in such an abrupt and undignified manner.

Sometimes frustrations we neither foresee nor understand seem to block our progress. When we hit God's obstructions, we tend to bumble up and down in confusion just like Mr. Bee. Determined and impatient, we repeatedly bump against God's will for us.

I had placed the window in the roof for a purpose far beyond Mr. Bee's power to comprehend. In the same way, the obstructions in our path may serve a purpose of God far beyond what our little minds can comprehend. As we make our plans each morning, let us allow room in our schedules for God's obstructions. What seems a senseless frustration to us may serve a profound and worthy purpose.

I sing thro' the shade and the sunshine,
I'll trust Him whatever befall;
I sing, for I cannot be silent:
My Father planned it all.

—H. H. Pierson

Sweet Will of God

1. My stub - born will at last hath yield - ed; I would be
2. I'm tired of sin, foot - sore and wea - ry; The dark - some
3. Thy prec - ious will, O con - qu'ring Sav - ior, Doth now em -
4. Shut in with Thee, O Lord, for - ev - er, My way - ward
Thine and Thine a - lone; And this the prayer my lips are
path hath drear - y grown; But now a light has ris'n to
brace and com - pass me; All dis - cords hushed, my peace a
feet no more to roam; What pow'r from Thee my soul can
Chorus
bring-ing,"Lord, let in me Thy will be done."
cheerme: I find in Thee my Star, my Sun.
riv - er, My soul, a pris - oned bird set free.
sev - er? The cen - ter of God's will my home.
Sweet will of God, still
fold me clos - er, Till I am whol - ly lost in Thee; Sweet will of
God, still fold me clos - er, Till I am whol - ly lost in Thee.

Words and Music by Mrs. C. H. Morris

The Disciplinarian

READ:
Luke 9:51–56

What will ye? shall I come unto you with a rod, or in love, and in the spirit of meekness? —1 CORINTHIANS 4:21

I was clearing some overgrowth with a tractor and mower when I saw a blur of movement at the edge of my vision. An instant later, pain exploded in my face as a yellow jacket plunged her stinger into my flesh, injected her venom, and zoomed away—all within a fraction of a second.

Her plan was simple, her strategy uncomplicated: she wanted me out of her territory, so she brought me an incentive to comply. And comply I did! I had one overpowering desire: to put the greatest possible distance between me and her in the shortest possible time.

In the reading above, James and John seemed to think a yellow jacket strategy would work well with the Samaritans. They thought the ideal response to the Samaritans' cold reception would be to call down fire from heaven on the offenders. But Jesus did not agree. "Ye know not what manner of spirit ye are of," He said.

How is it with our families? Are we ever tempted to use the yellow jacket strategy there? A proper balance of firmness and love will yield the wholesome fruit of godly discipline. If either of these elements is missing, the discipline will not have the desired result. With the yellow jacket I encountered, I got the distinct impression that she was a little short on love. Though I cooperated and left her territory, she is now more my enemy than ever.

On the other hand, love without firmness sends the signal that we are not committed to the requirement of obedience. Our goal in discipline is to bring about willing, cheerful, and respectful obedience. That is a level of cooperation the yellow jacket will never achieve.

A son may be spirited yet be submissive.
A dad must be loving but never permissive.

God, Give Us Christian Homes

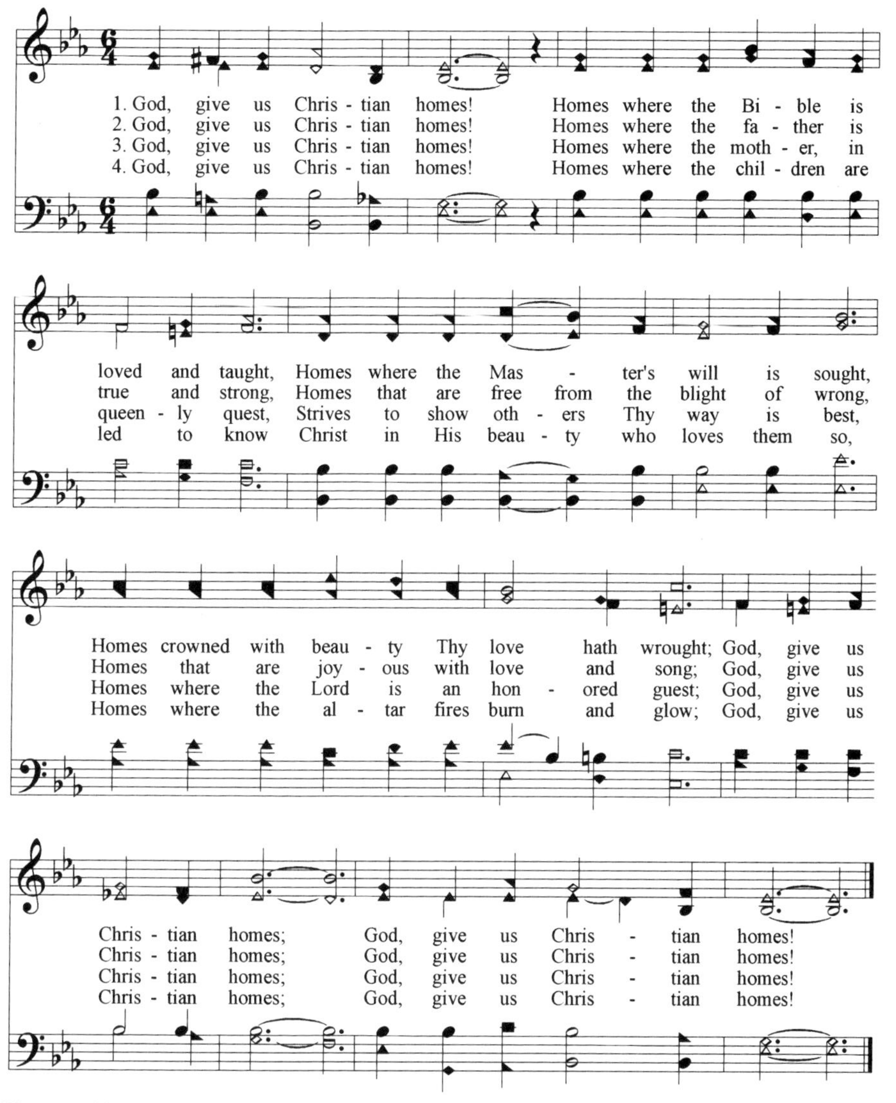
1. God, give us Chris - tian homes! Homes where the Bi - ble is
2. God, give us Chris - tian homes! Homes where the fa - ther is
3. God, give us Chris - tian homes! Homes where the moth - er, in
4. God, give us Chris - tian homes! Homes where the chil - dren are
loved and taught, Homes where the Mas - ter's will is sought,
true and strong, Homes that are free from the blight of wrong,
queen - ly quest, Strives to show oth - ers Thy way is best,
led to know Christ in His beau - ty who loves them so,
Homes crowned with beau - ty Thy love hath wrought; God, give us
Homes that are joy - ous with love and song; God, give us
Homes where the Lord is an hon - ored guest; God, give us
Homes where the al - tar fires burn and glow; God, give us
Chris - tian homes; God, give us Chris - tian homes!
Chris - tian homes; God, give us Chris - tian homes!
Chris - tian homes; God, give us Chris - tian homes!
Chris - tian homes; God, give us Chris - tian homes!

WORDS AND MUSIC BY B. B. MCKINNEY

Beautiful Boundaries

READ:
Proverbs 6:20–35

My son, keep thy father's commandment, and forsake not the law of thy mother. —PROVERBS 6:20

The man let his wife's hens out of the coop so they could enjoy a little freedom for the afternoon. He knew the hens would voluntarily go back into their coop at dusk. That evening he forgot to go check on the hens. In the meantime, a breeze blew the coop door shut. When the hens tried to go to roost, they found the entrance closed.

One by one the lights in the man's house winked out until it stood dark and silent. This was what the neighborhood dogs had been waiting for. Without further delay, they loped in the driveway to begin their nightly routine. First they checked the tires on the man's pickup truck for the latest community news, taking care to leave their own updates. Next they visited the back porch to clean up any leftovers in Moses' cat dish. Then the dogs went to the henhouse, where they discovered the night's bonanza.

The next morning the woman pieced together the sad events from the feathers strewn about. The man was remorseful, but it was too late to do what he had neglected the night before. He studied the coop mournfully. It was not beautiful, but it was secure. At times the hens seemed to think its confining walls interfered with their happiness; but he imagined that as the dogs closed in on them, they thought of the inside of that coop as the most beautiful place in the world.

Life is full of boundaries that may appear either burdensome or beautiful. If we wait to recognize their value until we are in the teeth of the enemy, we will have waited too long.

Walls are built both high and stout,
To guard what's in, exclude what's out.

Prick Up Your Ears

READ:
Psalm 34

Hear, ye children, the instruction of a father, and attend to know understanding. —PROVERBS 4:1

Unlike humans, the common housefly cannot gain wisdom. It spends its short lifetime reacting mindlessly to whatever happens around it. If the weather is cool, it instinctively seeks a perch on a ceiling or in a sunny spot. If it smells some juicy, rotten food, it buzzes over to investigate. If it senses the shadow of a descending flyswatter, it tries to fly away. But it demonstrates no ability to gain wisdom from life's experiences.

God will not let us humans off so easily. He created us with the ability to learn, and He has instructed us to put that ability to work seeking knowledge and wisdom. But far too many people are like the housefly: they spend much idle time living for the moment, not thinking ahead. You see them with electronic earbuds sprouting from either side of their heads, or video game controllers glued to their hands, or their bodies buried in sofa cushions and their eyes riveted to television screens.

Wasting time in pointless diversions is not God's will for godly people. God commands us to hear the instructions of fathers or teachers. The learner should "attend (prick up the ears) to know understanding."

Years ago I attended a driver education class in a local public high school. One day as we sat waiting for the class to start, the door opened and a student shuffled in. "I don't need this class; I already know how to drive," he declared. "I just need the paper to prove it." He later dropped out of the class.

May we never carry the attitude of that student. When we are presented with the opportunity to learn, let us prick up our ears, lean forward in our seats, and drink it in.

Prick up your ears and hear
The teaching clear of a father dear.

The Presumptuous Possum

READ: 1 Samuel 21

I pray not that thou shouldest take them out of the world, but that thou shouldest keep them from the evil. They are not of the world, even as I am not of the world. Sanctify them through thy truth: thy word is truth. —JOHN 17:15–17

The man and the woman lived in a big house. After the children were married, it was just the two of them—at least that's what they thought. They didn't find out when the possum slipped into the garage, sniffed out the bag of cat food, noticed that the pull-down stairs had been left down, and discovered how cozy the attic was. The possum knew instinctively that the man was his enemy, but this opportunity was just too good to pass up. It was like living in a grocery store with a climate-controlled bedroom. Life couldn't get any better than this for a possum.

At three o'clock one morning, the sleepless man wandered out to the back porch and discovered the possum helping himself from the cat's dish. The man watched with disgust as the ugly creature scuttled into his garage and disappeared into a hiding place. He determined to put an end to this creature's occupancy of his home. His house was big, but not big enough to be shared with a possum.

The possum was by no means the first to make the fatal mistake of becoming too much at home in enemy territory. When Christ was on trial, His disciple Peter followed "afar off." While his Lord stood cold and exposed before His accusers, Peter drew near to be warmed at the fireside of the enemy. It wasn't long before he had sworn that he did not know his Master.

How comfortable are we in this wicked world? Have we found a cozy spot in the enemy's territory as David did in today's reading? Are our bellies full of the world's philosophies? Is our time spent with the enemy's amusements? Beware! The enemy's camp is a dangerous place to make yourself at home. That was the last lesson the possum learned.

I am a stranger here, dependent on thy grace,
A pilgrim as my fathers were, with no abiding place.

—from the *Psalter* (#424 in the *Mennonite Church Hymnal*)

I Feel Like Traveling On

With feeling
1. My heav'n - ly home is bright and fair, I feel like trav - el - ing on,
2. Its glit - t'ring tow'rs the sun out - shine, I feel like trav - el - ing on,
3. Let oth - ers seek a home be - low, I feel like trav - el - ing on,
4. The Lord has been so good to me, I feel like trav - el - ing on,
Nor pain, nor death can en - ter there, I feel like trav - el - ing on.
That heav'n - ly man - sion shall be mine, I feel like trav - el - ing on.
Which flames de - vour, or waves o'er - flow, I feel like trav - el - ing on.
Un - til that bless - ed home I see, I feel like trav - el - ing on.
Chorus
Yes, I feel like trav - el - ing on, I feel like trav - el - ing
trav - el - ing on,
on; My heav'n - ly home is bright and fair, I feel like trav - el - ing on.
trav - el - ing on;

WORDS AND MUSIC BY WILLIAM HUNTER, D. D.
ARRANGEMENT BY JAMES D. VAUGHAN

Blinders

READAD:
Proverbs 5

I will set no wicked thing before mine eyes: I hate the work of them that turn aside; it shall not cleave to me. —PSALM 101:3

My wife and I had some business in Lancaster, Pennsylvania. We noticed with interest some sights that would seem very strange in Pantego, North Carolina. Among these were the many horse-drawn buggies. In every case, the horse's bridle was fitted with leather eye shields, called blinders, to block the horse's peripheral vision. There are things on the streets of Lancaster that are better for the horse not to see.

We appreciated that the folks of Lancaster sought to protect themselves and their horses by shielding their horses' vision. We wondered if these people also take measures to protect themselves by shielding their own vision. We did not see any humans wearing blinders, yet as we traveled through Lancaster, we did see things around us that would be better for a person not to see.

Wouldn't it be good for people to have blinders to guard their eyes from the blatant immodesty that abounds today? Or how about blinders for our wide-eyed children when we walk past the electronics section or the magazine racks at the store? We could even use blinders in our homes. As the poet says, "Let me be a little kinder, let me be a little blinder, to the faults of those around me." Yes, blinders like that would be useful indeed.

On second thought, most of us do wear invisible blinders. These blinders can cause husbands and wives not to notice one another's good points. Blinders can cause a father not to notice the crying heart of his son. Blinders can cause a mother not to notice that her daughter is yearning to ask a sensitive question.

May the Lord give us crystal clear vision where we need it, with wisdom to shield our eyes when it is necessary.

Purer in heart, O God, help me to be;
May I devote my life wholly to thee.

—Fannie Estelle Davison

Guide Me, O Thou Great Jehovah

1. Guide me, O Thou great Je - ho - vah, Pil - grim thru this bar - ren
2. O - pen now the crys - tal foun - tain, Whence the heal - ing wa - ters
3. When I tread the verge of Jor - dan, Bid my anx - ious fears sub -
land; I am weak, but Thou art might - y, Hold me
flow; Let the fier - y, cloud - y pil - lar, Lead me
side; Bear me thru the swell - ing cur - rent, Land me
with Thy pow'r - ful hand; Bread of hea - ven, Feed me till I want no
all my jour - ney thru; Strong De - liv'r - er, Be Thou still my strength and
safe on Ca - naan's side; Songs of prais - es I will ev - er give to
p
more: bread of hea - ven, Feed me till I want no more.
shield: strong De - liv'r - er, Be Thou still my strength and shield.
Thee; Songs of prais - es I will ev - er give to Thee.
f
3
4

WORDS BY WILLIAM HASTINGS
MUSIC BY THOMAS HASTINGS

Nest Building

READ:
Matthew 6:19–34

Behold the fowls of the air: for they sow not, neither do they reap, nor gather into barns; yet your heavenly Father feedeth them. Are ye not much better than they? —MATTHEW 6:26

My perspective: Some birds show a lack of discernment when they choose where to build their nests. A wren raised her family in the back bumper of our car. A roadrunner hollowed out a depression and laid her eggs in the gravel of our church driveway. Some barn swallows built their mud nest above the lintel of my front door.

Humans are much smarter than birds. People take great care in building a house. They may get a certified architect to design it and a building inspector to ensure that all phases of the construction comply with the building code. From the concrete foundation to the standing-seam metal roof, humans build so that their nests will be serviceable and hold their value for decades. I sure am glad I'm not a bird.

The bird's perspective: Some humans show a lack of discernment when they build their houses. A retired couple built a huge mansion after their children left home. Our nest is just the right size so that when it becomes overcrowded, our children are old enough to fly. No bird in its right mind would build a nest fifty times larger than it needs.

Birds are much smarter than humans. Some people don't even have enough money to build their nest. They take out huge mortgages and obligate themselves to large house payments for decades to come. If I had to bear such a heavy debt load, I wouldn't even be able to sing in the mornings. I sure am glad I'm not a human.

God's perspective: I created birds and humans. I gave the birds instinct to know how and where to build their nests. I bestowed on humans the powers of reason. Only the endowments of humans are coupled with accountability to their Creator.

Dear Lord and Father of mankind . . . Reclothe us in our rightful mind.

—J. G. Whittier

Dear Lord and Father of Mankind

1. Dear Lord and Fa - ther of man - kind, For - give our fool - ish
2. In sim - ple trust like theirs who heard, Be - side the Syr - i -
3. O Sab - bath rest by Gal - i - lee, O calm of hills a -
4. Drop Thy still dews of qui - et - ness, Till all our striv - ings
ways; Re - clothe us in our right - ful mind, In pur - er
an sea, The gra - cious call - ing of the Lord, Let us,
bove, Where Je - sus knelt to share with Thee The si - lence
cease; Take from our souls the strain and stress, And let our
lives Thy ser - vice find, In deep - er rev - 'rence, praise.
like them, with - out a word Rise up and fol - low
of e - ter - ni - ty, In - ter - pret - ed by love!
or - dered lives con - fess The beau - ty of Thy peace.

Words by John G. Whittier
Music by Frederick C. Maker

Who Owns the Barn?

READ:
Psalm 50

For every beast of the forest is mine, and the cattle upon a thousand hills. —PSALM 50:10

The carpenter bee is a fascinating little creature. Her stubby body appears anything but aerodynamic, yet she can hover, pivot, back up, and dart forward with amazing agility. But I would enjoy watching her and her kind a lot more if they would quit eating holes in my barn timbers. The holes she chews in my wood become nests for laying her eggs.

These bees are territorial, and each bee fiercely guards what she considers her property. That is what the hovering is all about. She challenges anything that flies near her nest—a butterfly, a wasp, or another bee can expect to be confronted. One astute little bee shot skyward in hot pursuit of a passing vulture. The message is unmistakable. "This is my property. Stay away."

If the carpenter bee could understand English or even Spanish, I'd like to ask her some questions. "Madam, how did this barn become your property? I paid thousands of my hard-earned dollars to have it built. I thought it was my barn. Why are you chewing holes all over something that does not belong to you?" I'd like to write her side of the imaginary conversation, but I cannot think of a single sane reason she might give for claiming my barn as her territory.

But listen. From somewhere I hear God's voice asking me, "Why are you claiming my barn as your own? Whose money did you buy it with? Where did you get the strength to earn that money? Who endowed you with the intelligence to even know you needed a barn? Who gave you the senses to watch the bees chewing holes and to listen to their buzzing?"

As I consider the matter, I cannot think of a single sane reason I might give for claiming God's barn as my territory.

The barn, the bee, and me belong to God, all three.

The Language of Crowing

READ: 1 Kings 20:1–21

Even so the tongue is a little member, and boasteth great things. Behold, how great a matter a little fire kindleth! —JAMES 3:5

If you listen in the dark stillness of the countryside some morning before dawn, you may hear the strident voice of a rooster crowing. It is a surprisingly loud cry, easily heard from one farm to the next. Only roosters and people speak the language of crowing. I do not understand exactly what a rooster means to say by his crowing, but it is not a humble sound. It sounds like a call for attention. Perhaps by crowing the rooster is notifying all other roosters within hearing distance that this is his farm.

I have a better comprehension of the language of crowing as it is spoken by people. The dictionary says that when people crow, they are usually gloating, boasting, or exulting. The encyclopedia says chickens are not very intelligent. I assume this applies to crowing roosters—and possibly to crowing people too.

The language of crowing is easy to learn; it is a language nearly all people can speak if they wish. However, the more we are governed by the mind of Christ, the less inclined we are to crow. The Bible has a good bit to say about crowing. It uses the term *boast,* which means the same thing. Today's key verse notes that our tongue is a small part of our body, yet it boasts great things. The Apostle Paul tells us in Romans 3 that boasting is excluded from the life of a spiritual person. That means there is no room for it. Let us avoid the language of crowing, preferring rather the meek, unassuming words of godliness.

If we crow, we do not know God's great disdain for all that's vain.

The Language of Hens

READ:
Proverbs 15:1–15

A soft answer turneth away wrath: but grievous words stir up anger.
—PROVERBS 15:1

Hens cluck, cackle, and squawk. Their clucking in particular can be quite expressive. Clucking is a murmuring, low-intensity language. By changing the tone of the clucking, hens can send communications that range from comforting, soothing messages to stern, rebuking disapproval.

Clucking changes to cackling when a situation like the laying of an egg calls for a more emotional response. Cackling in turn changes to squawking when the hen feels that events are spiraling out of her control. Hens' final communications are often done in the language of squawking.

People do not speak the language of hens—or maybe they do. God has created us, like clucking hens, with the flexibility to express great variations of meaning at low intensity, simply by changing the tone of our utterances. For example, consider the question, "Why are you crying?" We could ask this sympathetically, scornfully, rebukingly, teasingly, wearily, or disbelievingly by changing the tone of our voice.

In everyday language, some of the same words used for chicken communication are also applied to humans. The dictionary says clucking expresses interest or concern. Cackling is often expressed as sharp, harsh laughter. Laughter can be as gentle as the tinkle of chimes in a soft breeze or as bitterly sharp as a Montana blizzard.

Like hens, people often resort to squawking as events spiral out of control. It may be a mother's exasperated screaming at her uncontrollable child or a man's vigorous protest when his pride has been injured.

We should aspire to speak more of the language of gentle clucking. We have no need for the language of squawking, because when events spiral out of our control, our sovereign God still holds them firmly in His hand.

It's not just the words but the tone that we use
That may stir up a fight or the tension defuse.

The Language of Hooting

READ: 2 Kings 2:9–25

Honour all men. Love the brotherhood. Fear God. Honour the king.
—1 PETER 2:17

If you stand outside near a wooded area on a still night, you may hear the eerie cry of an owl. I do not understand what the owl is saying when it hoots, but when people hoot, the meaning is unmistakable: it is a mocking laugh that communicates scorn and derision. Few things are more painful than to be hooted at by other people. This language produces no good, and we should never speak it.

Hooting often focuses on some oddity of a person or group in order to belittle them. Children may hoot at one another, or even at grownups. Children need to be taught respect, or they will grow up to be adults who disrespect law enforcement officers and other authority figures. Respect is the foundation of law and order.

Another form of hooting is jokes that belittle certain ethnic or religious groups. Such jokes are not becoming to those who fear the Lord. Mutual respect, to the point of honoring and preferring others above ourselves, is to be the way of life among believers. This respect is rooted in Christian love for our fellow man, and it is the foundation for harmonious church life.

Satan knows the advantage he will gain if he can introduce disrespect among children and young people, and if he can convince parents and teachers to ignore this behavior. If we lose ground in this area, we will suffer serious consequences.

Let us leave hooting to the owls among the shadowy trees on dark nights.

Unless we're an owl, we should not hoot;
We must not allow any scorn to take root.

Dreading What's Ahead

READ:
Psalm 131

Are not two sparrows sold for a farthing? and one of them shall not fall on the ground without your Father. —MATTHEW 10:29

If wrens dread anything, it must be the day their babies tumble from the nest and try their wings for the first time. The air fills with plaintive cries of the terrified fledglings who are discovering that flying is harder than it looks. Mama and Daddy Wren rush frantically to and fro, screaming warnings and urging their offspring to flutter to safe hiding places. Somewhere not far away a big yellow tomcat might be pausing midstride, listening intently and licking hungry lips. Surely this must be the most stressful period in a wren's parenting.

But one could not detect dread or any other negative emotion in the wrens' cheerful commentary the morning their eggs hatched. There was never a hint of discouragement as the pair made tireless trips in search of food for their growing family. Not once did we see Mr. and Mrs. Wren peevishly taking out their stress on one another. They lost not a wink of sleep worrying about the future. How did they do it?

Wrens accept life as it comes to them. They do not waste time wishing things were different. They do not question God's wisdom in creating yellow tomcats. They do not complain about the primitive method they must use to gather food. No wren has ever indulged in futile bitterness against God. Wrens accept circumstances as they are.

Wrens stay busy with the tasks at hand. They do not nostalgically long for days past. They do not bury present realities in the oblivion of fleshly indulgence. They do not look for shortcuts or bypasses around future challenges. They do what needs to be done today.

The next time I am tempted to discouragement or dread, perhaps God will send a wren to perch on my window sill.

Trust and obey, for there's no other way . . .

—John H. Sammis

Trust and Obey

1. When we walk with the Lord In the light of His Word, What a glo - ry He
2. Not a shad - ow can rise, Not a cloud in the skies, But His smile quick - ly
3. Not a bur - den we bear, Not a sor - row we share, But our toil He doth
4. But we nev - er can prove The de - lights of His love Un - til all on the
5. Then in fel - low - ship sweet We will sit at His feet, Or we'll walk by His
sheds on our way! While we do His good will, He a - bides with us still,
drives it a - way; Not a doubt nor a fear, Not a sigh nor a tear,
rich - ly re - pay; Not a grief nor a loss, Not a frown nor a cross,
al - tar we lay; For the fa - vor He shows, And the joy He be - stows,
side in the way; What He says we will do, Where He sends we will go–
Chorus
And with all who will trust and o - bey.
Can a - bide while we trust and o - bey.
But is blest if we trust and o - bey.
Are for those who will trust and o - bey.
Nev - er fear, on - ly trust and o - bey.
Trust and o - bey, for there's
no oth - er way To be hap - py in Je - sus, but to trust and o - bey.

WORDS: J. H. SAMMIS
MUSIC: D. B. TOWNER

NATURE SETTINGS

The Maple and the Vine

READ: 2 Corinthians 6:14–18

Stand fast therefore in the liberty wherewith Christ hath made us free, and be not entangled again with the yoke of bondage. —GALATIANS 5:1

Since the ditch bank was hard to mow, it had become overgrown with weeds, vines, and small trees over the course of several years. One day, armed with a chain saw and trimmer, I tackled the overgrown bank. I found a maple sapling whose trunk was painfully knotted and twisted in a spiraling pattern. Encircling the tender trunk was a tough, ugly brown vine that had been restricting and contorting the tree's growth for many months.

This vine had not always looked so ugly. Back in those early days when the sapling was but a slender twig, the vine had emerged beside it, tender and beautiful. These two young plants must have been a striking pair growing up side by side—the sapling slim and straight, the vine delicate and leafy! Then the vine coyly brushed the sapling, slipping a curling tendril around its base. If the young tree had been capable of sensation, it might hardly have noticed the vine's encircling movement. It might even have enjoyed the companionable attention. As time went on, the vine strengthened and tightened its grip, even as the young maple struggled to grow and expand its girth, gradually becoming what it was when I found it.

We understand the wisdom of God's Word in 1 Corinthians 15:33, which says, "Be not deceived: evil communications corrupt good manners." The young maple had no choice who its companion would be, but we are free to choose. Let us do so with care.

Take care when choosing a friend, for he may determine your end.

The Language of the Sunrise

READ: Revelation 21

And the city had no need of the sun, neither of the moon, to shine in it: for the glory of God did lighten it, and the Lamb is the light thereof.
—REVELATION 21:23

There are some things you will never behold. You will never see a sunrise in the west. You will never see a failed sunrise in which the sun gets stuck on the horizon, lacking the power to heave itself above the rim of the world. You will never see a news item warning us that due to high energy demand, the sunrise will be thirty minutes late tomorrow morning and will shine at half power.

The sunrise speaks a language understood in every nation on earth. It expresses deep truths about God and the universe. Since the fourth day of creation, every single day has started with a sunrise. No sunrise has ever been prevented by a famine, earthquake, or hurricane. Even on days when we cannot see the sunrise, it is still happening right on time.

It is worth our while to study the language of the sunrise so we can understand its message every morning. Every sunrise demonstrates God's presence and teaches us about His character. It illustrates God's perfect consistency, His awesome power, His love of beauty, and His bottomless supply of inspiration, creativity, and originality. It speaks of His faithfulness and His provision.

Best of all, the sunrise reminds us that we may go to dwell with God someday in a land beyond the sunrise. In that heavenly place, there will be no sunrises, for there will be no need of the sun. God Himself will be the dazzling source of light, far surpassing the beauty of any earthly sunrise.

Come, my soul, thou must be waking;
Now is breaking o'er the earth another day.

—F. R. L. von Cantel

This Is My Father's World

1. This is my Fa - ther's world, And to my list'n - ing ears, All
2. This is my Fa - ther's world, The birds their car - ols raise, The
3. This is my Fa - ther's world, O, let me ne'er for - get That
na - ture sings, and 'round me rings The mu - sic of the spheres. This
morn - ing light, the lil - y white, De - clare their Mak - er's praise. This
tho' the wrong seems oft' so strong, God is the rul - er yet. This
is my Fa - ther's world, I rest me in the tho't Of
is my Fa - ther's world, He shines in all that's fair; In the
is my Fa - ther's world, In bat - tle we must trod Je -
rocks and trees, of skies and seas His hand the won - ders wrought.
rus - tling grass I hear Him pass, He speaks to me ev - 'ry - where.
sus who died shall be sat - is - fied, The king - dom turns back to God.

WORDS BY MALTBIE D. BABCOCK
MUSIC: TRADITIONAL ENGLISH MELODY, ARR. BY S. F. L.

Save Our Planet

READ:
Hebrews 1

For as in Adam all die, even so in Christ shall all be made alive.
—1 CORINTHIANS 15:22

On the bed at the motel was a little card with the hopeful message, "Save Our Planet." Closer inspection revealed more details in fine print. The card suggested recycling ideas such as hanging up your towel after each use so it could dry and be used again. Although these were common-sense ideas, saving our planet seemed like a pretty tall order.

The underlying philosophy of the message was humanistic and self-serving to the core. It implied that Earth is teetering in the balance, and man must gallantly ride to the rescue. And in the short term, it would allow the motel owner to pocket the savings of his guests' frugality. Here are three truths to consider:

First, our earth is not in danger of extinction. God has promised that while the earth remains, seedtime and harvest and the seasons of the year will not cease. Someday the earth as we know it will perish in a flaming holocaust, but it will not be man who lights the match.

Second, although we are accountable to be good stewards of our resources, man is far too small to do any significant thing to save this planet. In God's discourse with Isaiah, He reminded the prophet that all the nations are less than a drop in the bucket (Isaiah 40:15).

Third, although our planet is desperately needy, its greatest problems will not be resolved by recycling. The sin of mankind is the cause of most problems the world faces. Jesus Christ gave His life to provide our salvation. He alone can save our planet.

But do we not have a small part in God's great work? Yes, Jesus' parting instruction will keep us busy as long as we live. "Go ye therefore, and teach all nations . . . to observe all things whatsoever I have commanded you" (Matthew 28:19–20).

We have heard the joyful sound: Jesus saves! Jesus saves!

—Pricilla J. Owens

A Slimy Lesson

READ:
James 4:1–17

Draw nigh to God, and he will draw nigh to you. Cleanse your hands, ye sinners; and purify your hearts, ye double minded. —JAMES 4:8

It was Sunday morning, and I was dressed up in my Sunday best, which included a clean white shirt. It was not time to leave for church yet, so I decided to visit the neighbors. I crossed the ditch between our properties by stepping across on a plank that spanned the banks. As I attempted to step up on the far bank, I lost my footing and began to fall backward. I grabbed for some long weed stems, but they slipped out of my grasp. As I continued my backward and downward course, I grabbed wildly for something, anything to stop my fall.

All my efforts failed, and I continued my descent uninterrupted until I came to a stop sitting in twelve inches of muck and slimy water.

Some minutes later I stood dripping a murky puddle on the back porch. I opened the door and called to my wife, "Honey, can you come here a minute?" Her assistance, a hot shower, and a change of clothing combined to prepare me once more to go to church. My unexpected Sunday morning diversion left me thoughtful and a bit wiser.

How many saints dressed in righteousness have ventured out on the plank called Questionable and lost their footing? Though they grasped wildly at Face-Saving stems in an effort to reverse their downward course, they eventually hit Sin's Depth and were covered with slimy filth. How many have remained there, fearing to face the scrutiny of the Beloved? How many have courageously slogged back to be cleansed by the water of the Word and be re-clothed in Righteousness? How many have wisely avoided the questionable shortcuts by traveling the longer way called Tried and Proven? Those who travel this way may not realize what muck and slime they have been spared, yet they are blessed.

A just man falleth seven times, yet riseth up and forward climbs.

—adapted from Proverbs 24:16

God of the Universe

READ:
Luke 8:22–39

And he said unto them, Where is your faith? And they being afraid wondered, saying one to another, What manner of man is this! for he commandeth even the winds and water, and they obey him. —LUKE 8:25

Early on the morning of July 4, 2014, the center of tropical storm Arthur swept across eastern North Carolina, packing high winds and heavy rain. In the wee hours, the man stood in the shelter of the back porch watching the roiling clouds overhead for signs of a tornado. Powerful gusts howled through the treetops, sending leaves and small branches spinning to the ground. Bands of torrential rain contributed their din to the commotion. Pepper stood looking worriedly up at the man. He whimpered and crowded close to his master's feet. The surrounding turmoil left him feeling insecure, but he trusted his master to fix the chaos.

The man felt very small and helpless. He awakened the woman. "It's getting pretty rough out there," he said. She committed the storm to her Master and promptly went back to sleep. To be transported from dreamland to glory in the funnel of a tornado didn't seem like such a bad thing to her.

The next morning the sun broke through the scattering clouds to smile on the rain-drenched earth. Pepper was taking a nap on the porch, and the woman was still buried under a mound of covers, finishing a restful night. Pepper might think his master made the storm go away and put his world back in order, but Pepper's master knows he is much too weak and small to be worthy of such trust.

The man bowed in worship before the God of the universe within which last night's storm was nothing more than an imperceptible rustle. His faith was inspired, and his resolve was settled to cultivate simple trust in his Master.

Carest thou not that we perish?
How canst thou lie asleep,
When each moment so madly is threatening
A grave in the angry deep?

—Mary A. Baker (#219 in *Life Songs 2*)

A Shelter in the Time of Storm

1. The Lord's our Rock, in Him we hide, A Shel-ter in the time of storm;
2. A shade by day, de - fense by night, A Shel-ter in the time of storm;
3. The rag - ing storms may round us beat, A Shel-ter in the time of storm;
Se - cure what - ev - er ill be - tide, A Shel - ter in the time of storm.
No fears a - larm, no foes af - fright, A Shel - ter in the time of storm.
We'll nev - er leave our safe re - treat, A Shel - ter in the time of storm.
Chorus
O, Je - sus is a Rock in a wea - ry land, A wea - ry land, a wea - ry land;
O, Je - sus is a Rock in a wea - ry land, A Shel - ter in the time of storm.

WORDS BY VERNON J. CHARLESWORTH, ARR BY IRA D. SANKEY
MUSIC BY IRA D. SANKEY

The Leaning Pine

READ:
Matthew 25:31–46

If the clouds be full of rain, they empty themselves upon the earth: and if the tree fall toward the south, or toward the north, in the place where the tree falleth, there it shall be. —ECCLESIASTES 11:3

In August 2011, Hurricane Irene threatened eastern North Carolina with wind and water. I decided we should take precautionary measures and cut down a tall pine which leaned slightly toward our dwelling. My son-in-law, an experienced logger, thought the tree could be safely removed. He carefully cut through the base, notching here and leaving a bit of wood there. He inserted wedges to get the tree to fall in the right direction. The pine teetered uncertainly as we struggled desperately to apply enough pressure in those final moments to drop it away from the house. How thankful we were when it finally lay on the ground, rather than in our kitchen!

Like the pine, we grow leaning in one direction or another. At the end of life we will fall the way we have leaned. In the Judgment, God will send some to the right and others to the left. It will not be hard for Him to know which side a soul belongs on; He will simply note which way that person leaned in life. If one's inclination was toward God's Word and His righteousness, He will place that person on His right. If one has leaned toward the world with a longing eye and a grasping hand, that person will fall to the left.

So we live, our daily decisions building the case for our own judgment. And when Judgment Day arrives, there will be no wedges, no strategic cutting, and no pressure applied to overcome a leftward lean. Today is our opportunity. The Judge offers not only to help us identify any wrong leanings, but also to provide us the power to overcome wrong and begin leaning in the right direction. How just is our God!

Is my name written there, on that page white and fair?

—Mary A. Kidder

Is My Name Written There?

1. Lord, I care not for rich - es, Nei - ther sil - ver nor gold;
2. Lord, my sins they are ma - ny, Like the sands of the sea,
3. O! that beau - ti - ful cit - y, With its man - sions of light,
I would be sure of heav - en, I would en - ter the fold,
But Thy blood, O, my Sav - ior, Is suf - fi - cient for me;
With its glo - ri - fied be - ings, In pure gar - ments of white;
In the book of Thy king - dom, With its page white and fair,
For Thy prom - ise is writ - ten, In bright let - ters that glow,
Where no e - vil things com - eth, To de - spoil what is fair;
Fine
Tell me, Je - sus, my Sav - ior, Is my name writ - ten there?
"Tho' your sins be as scar - let, I will make them like snow."
Where the an - gels are watch - ing, Is my name writ - ten there?
D.S.– In the book of Thy king - dom, Is my name writ - ten there?
Chorus
D.S. al Fine
Is my name writ - ten there, On the page white and fair?

WORDS BY MRS. MARY A. KIDDER
MUSIC BY FRANK M. DAVIS

Song Index

A

A Charge to Keep I Have **33**
A Joyful Song **19**
A Shelter in the Time of Storm .. **139**
All Things Bright and Beautiful.... **9**
Angry Words................................. **97**
Are You Washed in the Blood? ... **27**
Awake, My Soul, Stretch
Every Nerve **65**

B

Be Not Dismayed Whate'er
Betide...................................... **51**
Blest Be the Tie That Binds **81**

C

Can You Count the Stars?............ **93**
Come, Ye Sinners.......................... **77**

D

Dear Lord and Father
of Mankind **123**

G

God, Give Us Christian
Homes **115**
Guide Me, O Thou
Great Jehovah **121**

H

Higher Ground **41**
How Sweet, How Heavenly **39**

I

I Am Trusting Thee, Lord Jesus .. **67**
I Feel Like Traveling On **119**
I Gave My Life for Thee **109**
I Have Decided to Follow Jesus .. **17**
I Need Thee Every Hour **49**
If Thou But Suffer God to Guide
Thee **75**
Is My Name Written There? **141**
Is Your Life a Channel
of Blessing? **25**
It Is Well with My Soul................. **21**

L

Let Him Have His
Way with Thee......................... **47**

M

More Love to Thee........................ **15**

My Faith Looks Up to Thee.........53

N

None of Self and All of Thee 85

O

O Master, Let Me Walk
with Thee 107

P

Prepare to Meet Thy God 89
Prince of Peace!
Control My Will.....................69

R

Rescue the Perishing...................83

S

Sweet Will of God.......................113

T

There's a Wideness
in God's Mercy 29
This Is My Father's World..........135
Trust and Obey 129

U

Under His Wings..........................37

W

While the Days Are Going By.....43
Wonderful Words of Life.............99

Y

Yield Not to Temptation.............31

About the Author

Gary Miller and his wife Marie live in a rural area of eastern North Carolina. They have seven children, all married, and thirty-five grandchildren. Observing God's creation and reflecting on animal behavior provide Gary with ongoing inspiration for his short stories and articles. Many of these have been published in *Beside the Still Waters* and other periodicals.

Gary is a partner in a family-owned garage door business founded by his father. Although Gary is still active, he is slowing down due to Parkinson's disease, with which he was diagnosed in 2007. He is the author of *Shaking Hands with Mr. Parkinson.*

Gary looks forward to hearing from his readers and can be contacted at garymiller@emypeople.net. You may also write to him in care of Christian Aid Ministries, P.O. Box 360, Berlin, Ohio 44610.

Christian Aid Ministries

Christian Aid Ministries was founded in 1981 as a nonprofit, tax-exempt 501(c)(3) organization. Its primary purpose is to provide a trustworthy and efficient channel for Amish, Mennonite, and other conservative Anabaptist groups and individuals to minister to physical and spiritual needs around the world. This is in response to the command ". . . do good unto all men, especially unto them who are of the household of faith" (Galatians 6:10).

Each year, CAM supporters provide approximately 15 million pounds of food, clothing, medicines, seeds, Bibles, Bible story books, and other Christian literature for needy people. Most of the aid goes to orphans and Christian families. Supporters' funds also help to clean up and rebuild for natural disaster victims, put up Gospel billboards in the U.S., support several church-planting efforts, operate two medical clinics, and provide resources for needy families to make their own living. CAM's main purposes for providing aid are to help and encourage God's people and bring the Gospel to a lost and dying world.

CAM has staff, warehouses, and distribution networks in Romania, Moldova, Ukraine, Haiti, Nicaragua, Liberia, and Israel. Aside from management, supervisory personnel, and bookkeeping operations, volunteers do most of the work at CAM locations. Each year, volunteers at our warehouses, field bases, Disaster Response Services projects, and other locations donate over 200,000 hours of work.

CAM's ultimate purpose is to glorify God and help enlarge His kingdom. ". . . whatsoever ye do, do all to the glory of God" (1 Corinthians 10:31).

The Way to God and Peace

We live in a world contaminated by sin. Sin is anything that goes against God's holy standards. When we do not follow the guidelines that God our Creator gave us, we are guilty of sin. Sin separates us from God, the source of life.

Since the time when the first man and woman, Adam and Eve, sinned in the Garden of Eden, sin has been universal. The Bible says that we all have "sinned and come short of the glory of God" (Romans 3:23). It also says that the natural consequence for that sin is eternal death, or punishment in an eternal hell: "Then when lust hath conceived, it bringeth forth sin: and sin, when it is finished, bringeth forth death" (James 1:15).

But we do not have to suffer eternal death in hell. God provided forgiveness for our sins through the death of His only Son, Jesus Christ. Because Jesus was perfect and without sin, He could die in our place. "For God so loved the world that he gave his only begotten Son, that whosoever believeth in him should not perish, but have everlasting life" (John 3:16).

A sacrifice is something given to benefit someone else. It costs the giver greatly. Jesus was God's sacrifice. Jesus' death takes away the penalty of sin for everyone who accepts this sacrifice and truly repents of their sins. To repent of sins means to be truly sorry for and turn away from the things we have done that have violated God's standards (Acts 2:38; 3:19).

Jesus died, but He did not remain dead. After three days, God's Spirit miraculously raised Him to life again. God's Spirit does something similar in us. When we receive Jesus as our sacrifice and repent of our sins, our hearts are changed. We become spiritually alive! We develop new desires and attitudes

(2 Corinthians 5:17). We begin to make choices that please God (1 John 3:9). If we do fail and commit sins, we can ask God for forgiveness. "If we confess our sins, he is faithful and just to forgive us our sins, and to cleanse us from all unrighteousness" (1 John 1:9).

Once our hearts have been changed, we want to continue growing spiritually. We will be happy to let Jesus be the Master of our lives and will want to become more like Him. To do this, we must meditate on God's Word and commune with God in prayer. We will testify to others of this change by being baptized and sharing the good news of God's victory over sin and death. Fellowship with a faithful group of believers will strengthen our walk with God (1 John 1:7).